MILLER'S
Antiques Checklist
VICTORIANA

Consultant: Eric Knowles
American Consultant: Nicholas Dawes

General Editors:
Judith and Martin Miller

VIKING
STUDIO
BOOKS

MILLER'S ANTIQUES CHECKLISTS: VICTORIANA
Consultant: Eric Knowles

VIKING STUDIO BOOKS
Published by the Penguin Group
Viking Penguin, a division of Penguin Books USA Inc, 375 Hudson Street, New York, New York 10014, USA
Penguin Books Ltd, 27 Wrights Lane, London W8 5TZ, England
Penguin Books Australia Ltd, Ringwood, Victoria, Australia
Penguin Books Canada Ltd, 10 Alcorn Avenue, Suite 300, Toronto, Ontario, Canada M4V 3B2
Penguin Books (NZ) Ltd, 182/90 Waitau Road, Auckland 10, New Zealand

Penguin Books Ltd, Registered Offices:
Harmondsworth, Middlesex, England

First American Edition
Published in 1992 by Viking Penguin, a division of Penguin Books USA Inc.

10 9 8 7 6 5 4 3 2 1

Edited and designed by
Mitchell Beazley Publishers
Michelin House
81 Fulham Road
London SW3 6RB

Series Editor	Frances Gertler
Senior Art Editor	Eljay Crompton
Art Editor	Al White
Illustrator	Simon Miller
Assistant Editors	Katie Martin-Doyle, Caroline Juler
Typesetter	Kerri Hinchon for Evolution
Production	Sarah Schuman

American consultant: Nicholas Dawes
The compilers and the publishers will be grateful for any information which will assist them in keeping future editions up to date.

Although all reasonable care has been taken in the preparation of this book, neither the publishers nor the compilers can accept any liability for any consequences arising from the use of, or the information contained herein.

Library of Congress Cataloging in Publication Data

Victoriana/consultant Eric Knowles; general editors, Judith and Martin Miller.
    p. cm - (Miller's antique checklists)
    Includes index
    ISBN 0-670-83262-6
    1. Victoriana – Collectors and collecting I. Knowles, Eric. II Miller, Judith. III Miller, Martin. IV. Series

Linotronic output by The Imaging Business, London N7
Reproduction and camera work by Scantrans Pte. Ltd., Singapore
Origination by Mandarin Offset, Hong Kong
Produced by Mandarin Offset. Printed and bound in Hong Kong

CONTENTS

SILVER AND METALWORK

TEXTILES

MISCELLANEOUS

HOW TO USE THIS BOOK

When I started collecting antiques, although there were many informative books on the subject, I still felt hesitant when it came to actually buying an antique. What I really wanted to do was interrogate the piece itself – to find out what it was and whether it was genuine. So we decided to produce our own series of books on how to do just that.

The *Victoriana* Checklist will show you how to assess a piece as an expert would, and provides checklists of questions you should ask before making a purchase. The answer to most (if not all) of the questions should be "yes", but remember there are always exceptions to the rule: if in doubt, seek expert guidance.

The book is divided into collecting categories, including furniture, glass, ceramics, sculpture, jewelry, silver, metalwork and textiles. It also looks at the enormous range of miscellaneous objects with which the Victorians so loved to surround themselves. At the back of the book is a glossary, bibliography and list of makers.

Experts are not made overnight: treat the book as a knowledgeable companion as you go around auction houses and antiques stores, and soon you will find that antique collecting is simply a matter of experience and of knowing how to ask the right questions.

JUDITH H.
MILLER

Each double-page spread looks at the work of an individual craftsman or factory, or a category of wares.

The first page shows a carefully chosen representative item of a type that can usually be found at antiques stores or auction houses (rather than only in museums).

The caption gives the date and dimensions of the piece shown, and a code for the price range of this type of article.

A checklist of questions gives you the key to recognizing, dating and authenticating antique pieces of the type shown.

PRESSED GL

A miniature Sowerby vase in gold vitro-porc, 1879; ht 4³/₁₆in/11cm; value code F

Identification checklist for Sowerby's vit
1. Has the piece a novel and decorative
2. Does it exhibit mould lines?
3. Are the motifs crisply executed?
4. Is the surface of the piece glossy?
5. Is the body almost opaque?
6. Does the piece have a trademark of a
7. Has it a Patent Office Registration m

Pressed glass
Press-moulding glass by mechanical means was one of the major achievements of Victorian glass makers. Most of the wares consist of domestic items such as drinking vessels, jugs, bowls, dishes, celery vases, salt cellars, and so on. These are usually made in clear, colourless "flint" glass. Coloured pieces, sometimes known as "slagware", tend to fetch higher prices.
Many of the designs imitated the fashionable and more expensive styles of cut glass. However, pressed glass motifs are regular but less sharp than in cut glass, and the seam lines made by joins in the moulds are often visible.

Pieces can be
as most carry
Design Reg
p. 184). The
difficult to se
detected by
the surface o
* Pressed gla
thickness wi
sometimes v
* Sculptural c
premium.

Lacy glass
This inexpen
machine-pre
in the United
is categorized
patterns. Piec
are in great d

40

Information helps you to detect fakes, copies and reproductions.

VALUE CODES

Throughout this book, the caption to the piece in the main picture is followed by a letter which corresponds to the approximate value (at the time of printing) of that piece

GLASS

Sowerby (English, 1847-1972)
Some of the best quality pressed glass, such as the piece shown in the main picture, was made by Sowerby's Ellison Glassworks in Gateshead on Tyne. They registered their products with the Patent Office from 1872 and introduced their peacock's head trademark in 1876.

The most sought-after glass is made of vitro-porcelain, which looks rather like porcelain or bone china, and was produced from 1877. It was manufactured in a wide range of colours, including cream (when it was called "Patent Ivory Queen's Ware"), white, gold, pale turquoise and jet (appearing black, but usually deep purple). The glass was also available in various marbled colours, such as purple, blue and green (malachite).

The Sowerby range consisted of vases, spill holders and wall pockets, small baskets, candlesticks and other ornamental items, and also ribbon plates and stands for dessert services. The designs were mostly in the 1870s and 1880s "Aesthetic" style, some in imitation of carved ivory and showing a Japanese influence; others derived from children's book illustrations by Walter Crane (1845-1915).

George Davidson (English, founded 1867)

Davidson's Teams Glass Works at Gateshead also produced a wide variety of useful and ornamental wares in clear and coloured glass. Their trademark was a lion above a crown within a circle, or from c.1880-90, a lion above a tower. This glass jug and tumbler was made in their "Pearline" glass, patented in 1889. Coloured blue or primrose, the patterns usually imitated the current fashion for "brilliant" cut glass.

Henry Greener (English, founded 1858)
From the late 1850s, this Sunderland works manufactured good quality clear and coloured glass. Like Davidson's, they produced many items to commemorate Queen Victoria's Jubilee in 1887, as well as other royal and historic occasions. Their

mark was a lion with a star, and after 1885, a lion with an axe. This pressed glass bowl was made to celebrate the Silver Wedding Anniversary of the Prince and Princess of Wales in 1888. The beaded lettering is characteristic of Greener's wares. It was also used by Davidson and copied on the Continent. The Continental pieces, which are unmarked, are of inferior quality.

Henry Greener, used 1875-85   Greener & Co. used c.1885-1900

Other makers
In Britain, high quality pressed glass was also made by the Manchester firms of Molineaux, Webb & Co., and John Derbyshire. In the late 1860s and 1870s, both companies issued designs in Greek key patterns, and star and leaf motifs with frosted effects that contrasted with the shiny body. Derbyshire also manufactured lions after the painter Sir Edwin Landseer, as well as figures of Britannia and Punch and Judy.
* The best known maker in the United States was the Boston & Sandwich Glass Company (1825-88), who specialized in the production of lacy glass.
* The most sought-after American pressed glass is commemorative.

41

INTRODUCTION

When Victoria ascended the throne in 1837 neither she nor any of her subjects could have imagined the extraordinary technological and scientific advances her reign was to witness, nor the huge explosion in population that occurred over the next 60 years. This led to the production on an unprecedented scale of a vast range of items in all media, many of them for the first time able to take advantage of new mass-production techniques.

The Victorian age witnessed a continuous transformation of the applied and decorative arts. The revived interest in Elizabethan and earlier medieval styles led to a Gothic Revival. However, many other styles proved popular such as Louis Quatorze, Renaissance and Jacobean. The influence of Japan and the Far East was also significant. Following their alliance in the Crimean War, links between the former foes, Britain and France strengthened, especially with regard to the arts, and French styles and products became an increasingly important influence on Britain and the United States.

During the 1950s and 60s Victoriana was disdained by antiques collectors and indeed the term was often used to describe any object considered by the arbiters of taste of the day as vulgar or at best incongruous. However, attitudes have changed since then, and many people now recognize the virtues of the products of the 19th century. Victoriana is enjoying an unprecedented level of respectability. Prices have risen and in some instances dramatically over the past ten or fifteen years, but there are still bargains to be found, making it possible to put together relatively inexpensively an interesting and attractive collection which should also in time prove to have been a good investment.

Although many people today shy away from the often imposing and bulky Victorian furniture, there is still a vast range of smaller objects – no other age was so obsessed with accumulating all manner of decorative and useful artefacts. Many collectors concentrate on a particular category of wares, such as china, glass or metalwork, but there is also an eager market for "theme" pieces such as commemorative items, folk art and so on. Victorian glassware, especially tablewares, moulded glass and the masterful art glass created in England, at Stourbridge, are currently inexpensive. Books from the period, such as volumes of the *Illustrated London News* or *Punch*, give a keen insight into the events and humour of the age and are often relatively inexpensive.

This book uses a broad definition of "Victoriana" and includes any item produced during the Queen's reign and typical of its day. More emphasis is given to peculiarly 19th century and Victorian Revivalist items than to those produced in traditional styles inherited from earlier periods.

ERIC KNOWLES

8

THE MAJOR EXHIBITIONS AND ARTS MOVEMENTS

In the early years of Victoria's reign, architectural and artistic styles were dominated by a firmly entrenched Neo-classicism inherited from the reigns of George IV and William IV. Gradually, a taste for Baroque themes and incidental ornamentation began to infiltrate design. The result was often a vulgarized form within which embellishment took precedence over form, to the extent that form was often lost in excessive decoration. Styles and period elements often became confused, resulting in elaborate hybrids of the Classical, Rococo and Baroque. As early as 1846, Henry Cole (a contemporary designer and artistic reformer, later knighted for his contribution to the organization of the Great Exhibition) had lamented a decline in the applied arts and set about bringing good design back into everyday objects. In 1847, under the pseudonym Felix Summerley, he founded Summerleys Art Manufacturers for the sole purpose of producing objects of integrated form and decoration.

The Great Exhibition

Conceived primarily as a boost to international trade, the Great Exhibition opened in Hyde Park, London on May Day, 1851. The largest international exhibition that had ever been held, it was housed in the original Crystal Palace – an entirely prefabricated glasshouse three times the size of St Paul's Cathedral and built specially for the occasion. The Royal Commission appointed to organize the event included Prince Albert, Sir Henry Cole and Lord Russell, the Prime Minister. All areas of international artistic and technical achievement were represented. Thirteen thousand exhibitors took part, of which half were British; other countries were allocated space on the basis of their size. Categories of exhibits included textiles, organic manufacture, agriculture, vitreous-ceramic manufacture, engineering and machinery, chemical manufacture, metallurgy, architecture, fine arts and music and agriculture. The applied arts were well-represented and, although the display of paintings was prohibited, the halls were filled with all manner of sculpture, jewelry, ceramics, cutlery and furniture. The British mastery of ceramics was evident, with wares by Worcester (see pp.66-7), the Staffordshire potters (see pp.60-1), and other ceramists on display. Majolica designed by Leon Arnoux for Minton (see pp.70-1) was much admired. Glasswares, particularly cut glass, were exhibited, amongst others, by Webb & Sons (see pp.38-9).

The furniture exhibited included the papier-mâché work produced by the firm of Jennens & Bettridge (see pp.14-15) and the Renaissance revival pieces of W. Gibbs Rogers. The innovative mosaic carpet, designed by the Yorkshire firm of Crossley, caused a favourable reaction, as did the Kashmiri carpets from Srinagar. Predictably, many pieces depicted the Crystal Palace, from chocolate boxes with embossed card lids to elaborate glasswares and papier-mâché items. American exhibits included *The Greek Slave*, a hugely influential sculpture by Hiram Powers.

Despite the range and quantity of exhibits, the event was seen by many as representing the nadir of stifling Victorianism, rather than the pinnacle of achievement in 19thC design. Particularly in the area of the applied arts, a reactionary demand for a simpler approach led to the growth of several new artistic movements that moved away from the smothering High Victorian style, and which were to have a profound effect on all areas of design throughout Victoria's reign.

The Philadelphia Centennial Exhibition
A comparable occasion in the United States, though not so momentous in terms of altering the taste of an age, was the Centennial Exhibition held in Philadelphia in 1876. Here was displayed the peak of the Renaissance revival, with everything on a huge scale, whilst also reflecting the modern mechanical influence. Neo-classical themes combined with modern American motifs to create a peculiarly American style – porcelain and glassware in classical shapes were decorated with historical scenes, patriotic eagles and profiles of George Washington, as well as North American animals, such as the bison, walrus and bighorn sheep. Tiffany silverware, already exhibited at the Paris *Exposition* and the Great Exhibition, attracted enormous attention. Some of the furniture exhibited followed closely the styles produced by English firms such as Gillow, Cooper and Holt, and Collinson and Lock. Indeed, a piece designed by T. E. Collcutt for Collinson and Lock was shown at the Centennial, and helped to set the style for the entire show, a style typified by straight lines, elaborate turning and inlaid marquetry panels incorporating various woods and brass, and surface carving.

The Gothic Revival
Not everything shown at the Great Exhibition was vulgarly over-decorated. The relatively simple, neo-Gothic furniture designs of A. W. N. Pugin (see p.16-17), exhibited in artificially constructed Medieval Courts and displaying intrinsically simple and solid lines, offered a much-needed alternative. This particular Gothic revival, which began as early as the 1840s, was the first of several new artistic movements to spring up in reaction to the excesses of the High Victorian style. Evident in the work of designers such as Bruce Talbert (see pp.20-1) and William Burges (see pp.18-19), the Gothic Revival was to have a profound effect on design in all areas of the applied arts throughout the rest of Victoria's reign.

The Oriental Influence
By the late 1860s and 70s European design began to show an Oriental influence, especially that of Japan, which had begun trading with the West in the early 1860s after many years in isolation. The designs of Christopher Dresser, in particular, reflect a first-hand appreciation of Japanese culture, acquired during his travels there in the 1870s.

The Aesthetic Movement

The Japanese taste was readily received by a growing number of people who regarded themselves as aesthetes, and who championed a conglomeration of styles generally termed the Aesthetic Movement, one of whose main advocates was the playwright and poet Oscar Wilde. The movement became a way of life for many of its followers, who had their own code of dress and were obsessed with symbolism. They rejected unnecessary ornament as vulgar, preferring the simple, often ebonized furniture produced by designers such as William Morris, whose company, Morris & Co, was considered the leading arbiter of taste and the most important retail outlet for furnishings in the Aesthetic style.

The Arts and Crafts Movement

The Aesthetic Movement eventually gave way to the Arts and Crafts Movement, the influence of which can be traced as much to the Continent of Europe as to Britain. Exponents of this style strove to incorporate the ideals of the hand crafts-manship of the medieval age into the 19thC world of the machine. To this end, numerous guilds were founded to practise traditional handicrafts and construction methods. Perhaps the most significant of these was Charles Robert Ashbee's Guild of Handicraft (founded in 1888), which produced items in silver and other media, all hand-made and lacking the clinical precision typical of a machine-finished piece. Many guilds were not successful, as their ideals proved incompatible with harsh economic realities. Indeed, it was the production in the early years of the 20thC by Liberty & Co. of a range of affordable, mass-produced silverware with a hand-finished effect that finally spelled the end of the Guild of Handicraft, who found themselves unable to compete. However, the influence of the Arts and Crafts Movement continued into the Edwardian years, practised at various establishments such as the Cotswold school of furniture design, founded in 1894 by Ernest Gimson and Sydney Barnsley.

Towards Art Nouveau

The Aesthetic style sowed the seeds for the Art Nouveau style that dominated the French decorative arts in the later years of the 19thC and was adopted in Britain and the United States in the early 20thC. Designs of this period are charac-terized by sinuous lines and the use of naturalistic elements. The move towards simplicity and the harmonizing of design and function prevalent in all these movements can even be seen to preview the Art Deco movement of the 1920s and 30s. In this respect, Christopher Dresser was probably the most revolutionary Victorian designer of all (see pp.130-1).

Collectors should bear in mind that traditionalist and Revival products continued to be made alongside the more innovative items that resulted from the new artistic trends – for example, the taste for the French Neo-classical and the revivals of the Renaissance and the Elizabethan and Gothic styles found a ready market throughout the 19thC.

FURNITURE

A Gothic-inspired mirror-backed sideboard, c.1870

At the beginning of Victoria's reign most homes contained furniture in a variety of styles, although tending predominantly to French Baroque, late Georgian or the somewhat heavier pieces produced during the seven-year reign of William IV. For the first few years of Victoria's reign furniture continued in the William IV style, although often with embellishments such as carving or inlay. The Victorians also embellished plain furniture of earlier periods.

During the 19thC the demand for furniture grew at an enormous rate as the population continued its rapid growth. Demand necessitated the introduction of mass-production techniques, and cottage industries were replaced by large manufacturers. Furniture makers were also able to take advantage of advances in technology – for example, by the Victorian period veneers could be cut by machine instead of by hand, leading to pieces of high quality produced in a relatively short time.

By the time of the Great Exhibition, furniture, like other media, had reached what many considered to be a low point: the taste for decoration had gone beyond control, and many examples exhibited were over-decorated, the form smothered by decoration and almost reduced to a skeleton for a mass of often indiscriminate and unnecessary embellishment. The great age of nostalgia had begun, but historical styles at this period were misinterpreted and had become confused, resulting in incongruous combinations – for example, of the Gothic and the Baroque. However, a reaction against this suffocating over-embellishment and lack of sensitivity produced a finer appreciation of the Gothic principles of simplicity, pioneered, amongst others, by Talbert, Burges and Pugin; the latter's most important commission was the interior decoration of the Palace of Westminster. Primarily architects, these designers created pleasing and inventive pieces of Victorian high Gothic, the demand on an ecclesiastical level for this style of furniture starting a trend in the general population.

With the growth of the Aesthetic Movement in the 1870s and 80s (see pp. 10-11) came the taste for ebonized furniture and simple forms, with decoration restricted to confined areas rather than all over. The Japanese influence was evident, in particular in the work of E. W. Godwin. The Aesthetic style was especially popular in the United States, where it was adopted with great success by designers such as the Herter Brothers.

During the 1890s furniture became heavier, under the influence of the Arts and Crafts Movement (see p. 11) and oak became the preferred wood for styles that looked back nostalgically to those of medieval England. The medieval creations of William Morris were particularly influential.

Alongside all these new trends, Georgian-style furniture continued to be in demand. This was often of a very high quality, sometimes even surpassing that of the 18thC originals. Among the principal makers were Edwards & Roberts. As the 19thC wore on, furniture began to be made in materials other than wood. Papier-mâché was popular (see pp. 14-15), although, being a fragile medium, not many pieces have survived. Metal also began to be used; previously it had been confined to garden furniture, but gradually it was introduced inside the home – for example, for beds and fireplaces.

New forms were also invented. With music as the focus of the evening's entertainment for the leisured classes, most drawing-rooms were equipped with a piano. The sheer size of the grand piano led to the development of a smaller upright version, which became hugely popular, and was often also used as a vehicle for elaborate decoration.

The davenport, a compact writing table with a sloping top and a chest of drawers below, was introduced at the end of the 18thC, but grew enormously in popularity during Victoria's reign. These pieces are among the most sought-after of all writing furniture today.

By the end of the reign the Art Nouveau influence was creeping in, and furniture by Liberty or in the Liberty style began to appear, often in oak with carved mottoes or applied beaten copper panels.

PAPIER-MÂCHÉ

Japanned papier-mâché chairs, inlaid with mother-of-pearl, made by Jennens & Bettridge c.1860; ht approx. 32in/81cm; value code D (for the pair)

Identification checklist for papier-mâché furniture
1. Is the decoration japanned on a black background (or, occasionally, burgundy or green)?
2. Is the piece hand-painted, with elaborate floral or landscape decoration, or possibly exotic birds?
3. Does painted decoration include gilt-work?
5. Are borders or rims edged in gilt scrollwork?
4. Is there any inlay, probably mother-of-pearl?
6. If a tray, does it have an ornate outline?

Japanning
Oriental lacquered furniture first became popular in Britain during the 17thC. Japanning was the English attempt at the Oriental technique, with heavy varnishing used to imitate lacquer. The method was not exclusively Victorian but had grown steadily in popularity since the Regency period. The process was particularly successful in the decoration of papier-mâché objects; thus the Victorian fashion for furniture constructed from papier-mâché also led to a widespread use of japanned decoration.

The Victorians applied the traditional methods of furniture construction and japanning to contemporary styles – the balloon-back of the chair in the main picture is characteristically Victorian.

Black is the most common background colour, although examples with deep burgundy or dark green grounds also exist. The popularity of the black background owes nothing to the death of Prince Albert; it was quite usual before the phase of national mourning that followed his death.

Decoration is painted. The flowers and vines of the chairs shown *above* are typical, although complete landscapes are also fairly common.

Note
The technique of japanning papier-mâché is different to that used to japan sheet metal (usually referred to as tole ware) and the two should not be confused.

Jennens and Bettridge
(English, active 1816-64)

In 1816, Aaron Jennens and T. H. Bettridge took over the successful firm of Clays of Birmingham, specialists in papier-mâché furniture, and so began the great age of japanned papier-mâché, with which their name is now synonymous. Their earlier pieces tend to be small, useful wares, such as bottle coasters (which were very popular at the time), writing slopes, jewelry, cabinets, glove boxes, fans and frames for miniature paintings and wax miniatures behind glazed windows. Later they produced some larger pieces, such as cabinets, writing slopes and dressing tables.

Probably the most popular japanned wares of the day were the large and often graduated sets of serving trays. These were both useful and decorative, although some, like the example *above*, with its sumptuous landscape, are so elaborate as to seem not intended for practical use. Like most paintings on papier-mâché furniture, they are not signed. Copies of subjects by Sir Edwin Landseer were also popular.

Trays tend to have an ornate outline, accentuated with gilded edging. The Roccoco scrollwork on this example is fairly common. The value of these trays is usually dictated by the quality of the painting and the condition in which they have survived (see *opposite*). More elaborate, decorative examples tend to survive in better condition, not having been subjected to the ravages of practical use.

Marks

Pieces by Jennens and Bettridge tend to be impressed on the reverse beneath a crown . Copies are easily distinguished from the genuine article by the inferior quality of their decoration. No other papier-mâché companies are known to have signed their wares.

The use of mother-of-pearl inlay in japanned furniture was introduced by George Souter, at Jennens and Bettridge, in 1825 and became extremely popular. The dressing table *above* is a typical example. It also shows the elaborate gilded scrollwork characteristic of Victorian japanning.
* Large papier-mâché furniture is rare. Bedsteads, in particular, are hard to find, as are whole suites of furniture; if in good condition these are relatively very valuable.

Papier-mâché pieces occasionally feature shellwork, like that incorporated into the writing slope, *above*. This piece was one of several made in conjunction with the Great Exhibition of 1851, possibly as a souvenir; hence the depiction of the original Crystal Palace in Hyde Park.

Condition

The condition of japanned papier-mâché furniture is a crucial factor in valuation. papier-mâché needs to breathe and is liable to crack and warp if not given sympathetic conditions; the effects of modern central heating can be devastating. Restoration is difficult and generally unsuccessful.

A. W. N. PUGIN

A burrwood sideboard with fruitwood inlay, designed by A. W. N. Pugin (and probably made by J.G.Crace) c. 1850; ht 75 1/2 in/192cm; wdth 81/206cm; value code B

Identification checklist for furniture designed by Pugin
1. Does the piece exhibit Gothic elements?
2. Are inlays used in preference to pierced work or carved decoration?
3. Are any minor details and joints hand-made?
4. Does decoration incorporate formal rosettes, flowering trails or linenfold details?
5. In any applied decoration, do brass, leather, steel or porcelain predominate?
6. Is the main wood oak?
7. If a chair, are the legs fairly short?
8. If a table, are any stretchers H-form, possibly incorporating column supports with multiple knops, and set fairly low to the ground?

Augustus Welby Northmore Pugin (English, 1812-52)
Pugin, more than any other designer, epitomizes the Gothic revival in Britain (see pp.10-11). He established a style that synthesized heavy Gothic decoration and useful Victorian forms to produce mainly solid, robust and utilitarian furniture which was nevertheless highly ornamented and usually of oak. His stringent insistence on following medieval styles was in keeping with the return to the forms and methods of construction advocated by many 19thC cabinet-makers. Pugin's furniture designs for private houses tended to use inlay rather than elaborate carving. He favoured fruitwoods for decorative contrast when inlaid – as in the sideboard *above*. His work was executed by various makers – the sideboard was probably by J. G. Crace, who also produced the designs of Godwin and Voysey (see pp.22-3 and 28-9).

Commissions

Pugin received most of his commissions from the wealthy and important, often for one-off commemorative pieces. These are much sought-after today, particularly if supported by documented evidence of the commission. His conversion to Roman Catholicism in 1835 led him to ecclesiastical commissions, and his altar and other furnishings can still be seen in several Catholic churches in the British Isles.

* If documented proof of Pugin's involvement in a piece is not available, a certain amount of research using exhibition, maker and store catalogues, and references in illustrated books and magazines might provide the necessary confirmation.

Recognition points

Typical decorative features of Pugin's work include:
* rosettes, particularly on the side supports of chairs and tables
* flower heads on serpentine stems
* steel pendant loop handles
* blind tracery and crenellated decoration (a typically Gothic feature)
* linenfold panelling
* pierced galleried top rail
* ornamented chamfered pillars
* inlay, usually of fruitwood but occasionally using metal. Inlaid designs often incorporate initials or, in commemorative pieces, coats of arms, dates and so on.

Chair legs are usually short. However, the chair, *above*, was designed by Pugin's son, Edward, whose work was strongly influenced by his father's, and the legs, or side supports, are longer than is to be expected of the elder Pugin's work. Typically, the chair appears to have been constructed entirely from wood, using pegs and wedges in an almost medieval style of craftsmanship. This example is also plainer than one might expect of Augustus's designs, with decoration restricted to the form itself and the pierced supports and central seat rail.

The simple, solid lines of the desk, *above*, typify Pugin's sympathy with Gothic ideals of design. It displays the linenfold panelling, chamfered and carved uprights and foliate motifs characteristic of his work. Other versions exist, including one commissioned in 1849 to be the Prime Minister's desk at the Palace of Westminster.

* On tables, Pugin favoured H-stretchers and column supports with multiple knops.

A painted bookcase made to a design by William Burges
c.1860; ht 72in/183cm ; value code B

Identification checklist for the furniture designs of
William Burges
1. Is the piece Gothic in appearance?
2. In decoration, is use made of inlay, particularly of
ivory, or of colourful paintwork or gilding?
3. Does the piece feature any medieval carved motifs –
for example, crenellations?
4. Does the outwardly medieval appearance belie a
19thC function?
5. Is the piece ebony or, alternatively, ebonized?
6. Is the form solid?

William Burges (English, 1827-81)
Primarily an architect, Burges was a designer in the early Gothic style. He designed an enormous array of items – for example, cutlery, scent bottles, jewelry, metalwork and furniture – as well as buildings, including cathedrals and castles.

Most of his furniture was of pure Gothic form, colourfully painted and gilded with medieval characters and motifs. He also designed pieces in the Moorish and Persian styles. Burges applied medieval decorative elements to everyday Victorian furniture – for example, the bookcase in the main picture is very much a 19thC type of object executed in a medieval manner. Burges's medieval furniture tends to be very simple in construction. He favoured ebony or, alternatively, ebonized wood, as a basic material, although examples of his work exist in other woods.

Decoration

Decoration – painted, carved, or inlaid – is generally ornate and colourful, and the forms themselves can be elaborate. Carved decoration is usually flamboyant and includes crenellations, crockets and other medieval motifs. Although the bookcase is unusual in its lack of carving, its use of painting – in this case, classical and medieval figures – is typical. Several artists assisted in the decoration of Burges's designs. They include: E. J. Poynter, Sir Edward Burne-Jones, Simeon Solomon, Thomas Morten, N. H. J. Westlake, W. F. Yeames, Henry Holliday, J. A. Fitzgerald and H. Stacy Marks. Often several artists collaborated on a piece – indeed, a bookcase exists that displays paintwork by all those mentioned above.

Inlay is the most common form of decoration on Burges's work, in materials such as ivory, mother-of-pearl, cedar and boxwood. Ivory banding is also typical.

The ebonized table *above* was designed by William Burges for the Summer Smoking Room at Cardiff Castle, home of the Marquess of Bute (a long-standing patron of Burges's), a commission for which his brief was "Jacobean in shape, Romanesque in decoration". The Smoking Room is undecorated, which may explain the comparative simplicity of the piece.
* None of Burges's pieces are signed; they can generally be attributed only by accompanying documentation. However, where such provenance is unavailable, it is important for collectors to familiarize themselves with the tell-tale signs of his style – for example, the black and white chequered effect on the arched end-supports of the table and on the legs, created from ivory-inlaid ebony.

GAULBERT SAUNDERS
(English, dates unknown)

Like the furniture designs of Burges, the work of Gaulbert Saunders is influenced by the Gothic. The similarities between the two – who occasionally worked together – are evident when this hand-made cabinet, made to a design by Saunders, is compared to Burges's bookcase shown in the main picture. Saunders's cabinet makes use of Neo-gothic forms embellished with highly decorative inset panels depicting medieval figures and stylized floral decorations that bear a striking resemblance to those of Burges's piece. The linenfold panels are a common Gothicizing device, being an amalgam of early and late Gothic decorative styles (linenfold first appeared in the 14thC).
* Panels with floral decoration are often found on Saunders's pieces, although these seem to be more inspired by the symmetry evident in Isnik tile paintings than the Gothic.
* Unlike Burges, Saunders tended to sign his pieces, often flamboyantly. This cabinet has "Gaulbert" and "Saunders" carved in Gothic script just *above* the linenfold panels.

Availability

To a large extent, the work of both Burges and Saunders tended to be the result of commissions from wealthy clients. As a result, examples of their designs rarely come up at auction and are generally expensive.

BRUCE TALBERT

The Juno *cabinet, a fine ebony sideboard made to a design by Bruce Talbert c.1880; ht 91in/231cm, wdth 81in/206cm; value code A*

Identification checklist for the furniture designs of Bruce Talbert
1. Is the piece of very high quality?
2. Is the form strongly architectural?
3. Are Gothic-style pieces decorated with a cable motif, or possibly sunflowers?
4. Is use made of panel-form decoration?
5. Are any stretchers low on the ground?
6. Is the piece of mahogany, oak or ebony?
7. If ebony (or ebonized), does it feature profuse and elaborate inlaid decoration?

Bruce Talbert (Scottish, 1838-81)
Born in Dundee, Talbert trained as an architect, moving to London in 1865 to design furniture for Holland & Sons. His designs tend to be massive and often profusely inlaid, with ivory, marble and mother of pearl, and to display elements of both the Neo-gothic and the Aesthetic styles in varying degrees. The sideboard *above*, which derives its title from the

portrait of Juno inlaid into one of the five panels in the superstructure, represents an Aesthetic extreme, with its use of ebony, coupled with ivory and inlaid marquetry panels; the Gothic element is represented by the arches and Renaissance-style panels. This particular piece was designed for exhibition, which may partly explain the elaborate decoration, but it is by no means exceptional in Talbert's oeuvre.

Makers

The *Juno* cabinet was made by Jackson and Graham of Manchester, but Talbert also designed for Holland & Co., Collinson & Lock, and Gillows & Co. Some of his textile and wallpaper designs were produced by Jeffrey & Co.

The Jacobean influence predominates in the design of this piano. The base is solid and simple, with the low stretchers characteristic of many of Talbert's designs. The sunflower motif carved in the panels and on the legs, used originally in the 17thC, was revived by Aesthetic designers – it appears often on Talbert's work, as does the cabling found between the carved panels.

Marks

Talbert's pieces are not marked and are not as well-documented as the work of other designers. Some items are recorded by the maker – inlaid in the lid of this piano is the legend "Case by Gillow & Co Works by Erard". Some auction catalogues attribute pieces to Talbert without definite proof.

CHARLES LOCKE EASTLAKE (English, 1836-1906)

Like Talbert, Charles Eastlake trained originally as an architect, although he never practised. His theories of design, outlined in his book *Hints on Household Taste* (published in England in 1868), found an immediate following in Britain and subsequently in the United States, where his influence on furniture design was profound and where his name is still synonymous with the Gothic revival. His designs are similar to those of Talbert, but tend to be somewhat more rustic. His second book, *A History of the Gothic Revival in England*, appeared in 1872, and it is mainly upon the strength of these two volumes that his reputation rests. Another advocate of the Early English style, he deplored the shoddiness of mass-produced furniture, and his own designs tend to be heavy and solid. As with the designs of Godwin (see pp.22-4), decoration is generally restricted to simple turning, as on the oak day bed *below*. This piece is designed for comfort and function and its simplicity would have been unusual for the time. Comparison with the extravagance of the *Juno* cabinet gives an idea of the extreme range of styles of the period.

* As well as the furniture for which he is most famous, Eastlake also designed wallpapers, textiles, metalwork, interior fittings and jewelry.

* Eastlake's designs are not marked, and much is attributed to him, some of it erroneously. Some documented proof can be gleaned from the records of contemporary cabinet makers but, as his pieces are not stamped, even by makers, this could be a laborious process.

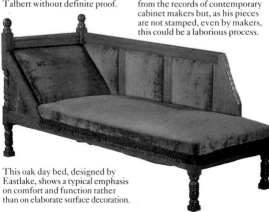

This oak day bed, designed by Eastlake, shows a typical emphasis on comfort and function rather than on elaborate surface decoration.

EDWARD WILLIAM GODWIN

An ebonized side cabinet after a design by E. W. Godwin
c.1870; ht 78in/197cm, wdth 50in/129cm; value code B

Identification checklist for Godwin's furniture designs
1. Is the piece ebonized?
2. Does it display a Japanese influence (see facing page)?
3. Are any door panels of a cruciform (cross-shaped) type?
4. Are chair stretchers diagonal with tapering spindles?
5. Is the piece in rosewood (rather than mahogany)?
6. Does any surface decoration include formalized flower heads, symmetrically arranged?
7. If a cabinet, does it have an open top rail, possibly with supports standing proud of it?
8. Are any hinges exposed and any handles or other fittings made into a decorative feature?
9. Is any metalwork decoration gilded?
10. Is a Greek key-type motif evident?

Makers
Godwin's furniture designs were executed by a number of cabinet makers. His longest association was with William Watt, who was responsible for the side cabinet *above*. Other makers were Collinson & Lock, who produced the octagonal rosewood table on the facing page, and J.G. Crace.

E.W. Godwin (English, 1833-86)

Initially an architect, Godwin's move to London at the age of 32 coincided with his diversification into interior design – as well as theatre sets and costumes, he designed textiles, wallpaper and furniture, including tables, chairs, cabinets, easels, shelves and bookcases. An exponent of "art furniture", a style popular within the Aesthetic movement (see pp.10-11), he was much influenced by the Oriental style, and was a pioneer of the "Japanesque" in Britain, a style epitomized by the chair *below*. Despite the fact that his pieces were hand-made, they were produced in quantity, although never mass-produced. His cabinets, which are fairly rare, tend to feature door panels with quartered fronts and broad strapwork hinges – no attempt is made to disguise or hide them. The example here demonstrates these, as well as the characteristic top rail, or gallery, with supports standing proud of the rails.

As well as ebony Godwin also worked in rosewood, from which the table *above* was made, and tended to avoid using mahogany. This table is stamped with the maker's mark, "Collinson and Lock London 5770", and a design number. Where pieces are attributed, it is usually to the maker; none of the items bear Godwin's name. Attribution to Godwin is based on stylistic similarities to his few known pieces or to surviving sketches by him: a drawing for a table similar to that shown here is in the Godwin sketchbook at the Victoria and Albert Museum in London, dated November 1872.

Godwin's interest in novel construction techniques is shown in this chair's finely-turned stretchers which radiate from a central cruciform block – also a feature of some tables (see *right*). Sometimes the stretchers have multiple knop spindles.
* Godwin's chairs, although not common, are more readily available than his cabinets. On some the seats are of rush rather than wood.

What painted or stencilled decoration exists in Godwin's work tends to be limited to symmetrical and stylized flower heads and geometric designs. These can be seen clearly on the hinged frame of the ebonized wood easel, *above*.
* Ebonized furniture cannot easily be restored, so the value of any piece will be dictated by the amount of original finish that it has retained.

MORRIS & CO.

*A fine Morris &Co. mahogany and satinwood buffet
c.1899; ht 48in/122cm, width 73in/186cm; value code C*

Identification checklist for the traditional drawing room
furniture of Morris & Co.
1. Is the piece solid and heavy?
2. If large, does it exhibit an architectural form?
3. Is it inlaid, possibly with satinwood?
4. Is it of very fine quality?
5. Is it mahogany?

Morris & Co. (English, 1861-1940)

Established originally as Morris,
Marshall, Faulkner and Co., this
association of like-minded
craftsmen advocated simplicity
and good quality handcrafting in
furniture construction. Having
been the main designer since its
foundation, William Morris took
sole control in 1875, and the
company adopted the name by
which it is still known today. Two
distinct and different styles can be
seen in Morris & Co. furniture of
this period. The checklist *above*
relates to the earlier, more
traditional designs, which tended
to be heavy and solid, made
principally from mahogany, and
inlaid, usually with satinwood.
Later pieces, exemplified by the
breakfront dresser on the
following page, tended to reflect
styles popular during the 17th and
18thC, being generally more
elaborate in both design and
decoration than earlier pieces.

The Sussex chair

The simplicity of traditional
pieces, such as the Sussex chair,
shown *above*, had wide appeal. In
the 1880s Morris & Co produced a

series in this style, which remains their most famous design. This example harks back to the rustic style popular earlier in the century, with its spindle back form and traditional woven rush seats. Typically, decoration is minimal, restricted to simple turned wood spindles. (Front legs sometimes incorporate bobbin turning.) Multiple stretchers have been added for strength. The chair was mass-produced, although hand-made for the most part, in line with the ethos of the Arts and Crafts movement, which shunned the use of machines in manufacture. The Sussex chair was still being manufactured in the early years of this century, despite the fact that, by the 1890s, new furniture designs by Morris & Co. tended to be far more sophisticated.

Later pieces often reflect an Italian influence. Mahogany is still used, with satinwood inlay, but designs tend to be more architectural and decoration more elaborate. Doors are glazed, and pierced carving is evident, particularly of any raised pediments, as in the breakfront dresser *below*. However, the effect is modest when compared to the excessive ornament of pieces by other contemporary designers. Such large items are almost too big for modern houses, hence smaller pieces are more sought-after and generally more expensive.

Marks

Pieces are almost without exception marked, generally with the "Morris & Co." stamp. Some also carry a registration mark – the buffet in the main picture is stamped "Rd. 352365". Makers are not credited.

Many Morris designs were widely copied – for example, the Sussex chair, but the Morris stamp is not known to have been faked and is therefore confirmation of originality. Collectors should beware of labels attached to some heavy oak furniture of Arts and Crafts inspiration which may say "in the style of M and Co" – such items are only copies.

Designers

Although William Morris was the main designer for the company in the early years, he later diversified into textiles (see pp.154-5) and furnishings, leaving the firm's furniture design to a number of others, including:
* Philip Webb (a founder designer-member of the company)
* Ford Madox Brown (again, an early associate)
* George Jack (who became chief designer in 1890, responsible for many of the mahogany inlaid pieces in the quasi-18thC style)
* W.A.S. Benson (who specialized in metalwork design and was responsible for the metal mounts on many pieces, such as the mahogany buffet).

A. H. MACKMURDO

*A Century Guild mahogany cabinet designed by Mackmurdo
c.1886; ht 86in/217cm; wdth 118in/299cm; value code A*

Identification checklist for furniture by Mackmurdo
1. Does the piece have a strong architectural feel,
particularly in any pediments?
2. Does any decoration consist of painted panels, or
incorporate organic motifs, such as leaves and flowers?
3. Is the standard of cabinet-making high?
4. Is the piece fairly solid in appearance and
construction?
5. Is a decorative feature made of any wood grain?
6. Are any brass fittings discreet?
7. Is the piece mahogany?

**Arthur Heygate Mackmurdo
(English 1851-1942)**
Having begun his career as an
architect, Arthur Mackmurdo
believed that responsibility for the
decorative crafts should be
restored to the artist from the
tradesman, and to this end, in
1882, he founded the Century
Guild, the first of the English Arts
and Crafts societies of designers,
artists, architects and
metalworkers. Mackmurdo's

furniture was created in the
workshop using a combination of
the talents of different craftsmen:
the mahogany cabinet *above*, was
designed by Mackmurdo but
features, on the doors and
drawers, cast bronze figurative
finger plates which, although
small and unobtrusive in the
manner of Mackmurdo's fixtures
and fittings, were probably by
Benjamin Creswick, a fellow
member of the Century Guild.

Style

Mackmurdo's work shows a distinct transition from the earlier, High Victorian mode to a simpler, more traditional style based on solid craftsmanship. The mahogany cabinet on the previous page is characteristic of his later work in its lack of elaborate decoration and its reliance on the colour and graining of the mahogany for much of its effect; this is particularly evident in the alcoves and panelled doors at the bottom. Organic elements are introduced into the details – the columns on the cabinet terminate in capitals decorated with pods and leaves.

Mackmurdo's forms usually have original elements, despite their basic adherence to tradition. This tall mahogany cabinet pre-empts the work of Voysey (see pp.28-9) with its vertical emphasis and long, slender, tapering legs. The painted panels, featuring typically late 19thC organic motifs of leaves and flowers, are probably by Selwyn Image, a co-founder of the Century Guild. The piece is marked "E.Goodall & Co. Cabinet Manufacturers 15 King St. Manchester", the makers of many Mackmurdo designs.

The distinctly organic feel of the chair *above*, from c.1880, is created mainly by the pierced carved back splat, which is made the focal point in an otherwise very traditional design. The flowing lines of the design give an early hint at the Art Nouveau style to come, as do the swollen legs supported on spade feet.

Textiles

With Herbert Horne, another Guild member, Mackmurdo designed printed textiles, produced for the Guild by Simpson & Godlee of Manchester, and woven fabrics, produced by A. H. Lee of Birkenhead.

MACKAY HUGH BAILLIE-SCOTT (English, 1865-1945)

Like Mackmurdo, Baillie-Scott was primarily an architect, and his furniture tends to be architectural in its execution. Working predominantly in oak or inlaid mahogany, the form of his pieces is original, even revolutionary, turning a functional item into an art object. Overall design is generally simple, often with the main decorative emphasis being on the wood grain. Simple chequered stringing or panelling is occasionally used. Overhanging pediments and spreading feet are characteristic. Much of his work was done to commission and included interesting designs for keyboard instruments. His work was particularly popular in Germany, where it still commands a high price.

C. A. VOYSEY

An oak settle by J.S. Harvey, made to a design by Charles Annesley Voysey c.1900; ht 72in/183cm; wdth 72in/183cm; value code A

Identification checklist for furniture designed by Voysey
1. Is the form highly individual, with a vertical emphasis?
2. Is any decoration pierced, possibly with a heart motif?
3. Is the principal wood oak?
4. If the piece is a large item of case furniture, does it have an overhanging top?
5. If a chair, are feet either clubbed or faceted?
6. If a chair, is there a rush seat, or evidence of any original seat having been rush?
7. Is the piece hand-made?

Charles Annesley Voysey (English, 1847-1941)
Originally trained as an architect, and much influenced by the Arts and Crafts Movement (see p. 11), Voysey designed for specific interiors and for interiors in general – including wallpapers and textiles. As well as furniture, toward the end of the century he also began to design household items, such as cutlery, tea wares, pen trays and clocks. Much of his work was commissioned and was invariably hand-made. Pieces are not marked but are well-documented; many are registered

at the Patent Office in London. The settle in the main picture has several typical features:
* stick splats
* high chamfered pillared sides
* prominent brass handles
* a vertical emphasis.

Note
A feature often associated with Voysey is the heart-shaped detail which is usually inlaid, as in the settle pictured here. However, it is not exclusive to Voysey and its presence is not therefore proof of his handiwork.

The strong vertical element of the oak chair, *below*, is typical of Voysey's designs. Modified versions appeared at the Arts and Crafts Exhibition in 1900, and subsequent examples with shorter backs were later produced for Liberty's. His chairs have usually either four stretchers, as here, or none at all. Rush seating is a common alternative to the fitted cushion.

In true Arts and Crafts style, construction is the most important decorative feature of this rare oak mantel clock, *above*. Beyond the natural grain of the wood, there is little extraneous decoration. The same design was later manufactured in aluminium by W. H. Tingey.

Voysey often used panels to break up large expanses of case furniture, as in the rosewood piano, *below*. The heart motif is again prominent.

Value point
Clocks and pianos of the period need not be in working order. They are sought-after today for their decorative appeal.

JOHN HENRY BELTER

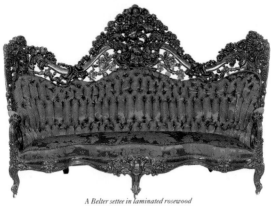

A Belter settee in laminated rosewood
c.1856; lgth 91in/231cm; value code A

Identification checklist for Belter furniture

1. Is the piece constructed wholly or partially, of laminated rosewood?
2. Are the laminated components curved and at least one inch (2.54cm) thick with at least six distinct layers?
3. Is the ornamental carving extensively pierced?
4. Are the proportions grander than in comparable European furniture?
5. Is the carving well executed and extravagant?
6. Does the graining of each layer run in the opposite direction to its fellow?

John Henry Belter (The United States, 1804-63)

The German-born cabinet maker, John Henry Belter, gave his name to a style of American furniture that was especially popular in the mid-19thC. By the 1840s, the designer had assumed the title of "America's most fashionable cabinet-maker" and when he died, the "Belter style" applied to any large-scale, elaborate Rococo furniture, whether or not it was made by his firm.

Belter emigrated to the United States in 1833 and developed a range of sumptuously carved and heavily proportioned pieces that were designed to grace the urban and suburban houses of the country's nouveau riche.

His company continued to trade under his name until 1863 when it was taken over by his brother-in-law and became known as Springmeier Bros. This firm ceased trading in 1867.

Belter's furniture was rarely exported and is hardly ever found outside the United States. It was particularly fashionable in the French-speaking communities, notably New Orleans, New York City and Baltimore, which were populated by wealthy Parisian exiles after the revolution of 1848.

The Belter style went out of fashion in the 1870s, but some of the designs are now highly collectable. They include the most elaborate pieces, especially rare forms such as tables or wares which are decorated with figural motifs including portrait images of famous historical personalities.

Marks

Belter furniture is seldom marked, although some examples are inscribed "J.H. Belter & Co." in black ink on the frame. Printed labels are also occasionally attached.

Types of furniture

Typical products of Belter's New York workshops were "parlour suites" which consisted mainly of a sofa or *méridienne* (chaise longue), armchairs, up to eight side chairs, piano stools, centre tables, side or console tables, toilet or dressing tables, beds, firescreens and *étagères* (whatnots, or stands). The settee in the main picture is a particularly fine example of Belter's "Rococo revival".

Decoration

Pieces were usually intricately carved and pierced, and included flora, fauna, foliate and Baroque scrollwork. Occasionally, Belter gilded the carving.

was built up from at least six (and sometimes as many as sixteen) individual layers. Seven layers are common in side chairs but more complex forms such as sofa backs and bed headboards often include as many as between ten and eighteen layers.

On drawer fronts and other flat surfaces, Belter frequently employed a four-layer laminate in place of a single sheet of veneer. The laminate was both flexible and tough, and it was especially suitable for carving.

He reserved the laminates for his solid, carved components, using indigenous American woods with decorative graining – for example, maple, for drawer interiors.

Belter designed this open armchair in c.1850. It illustrates his predilection for "Rococo" patterns of realistic flowers and fruit, and is made of laminated rosewood. In his later work, Belter often used black walnut, and other examples were ebonized.

Techniques

From the mid-19thC, Belter's favourite material was laminated rosewood. His patented techniques involved gluing together long strips of veneer (usually rosewood) which were then steamed, compressed and moulded into forms that were especially suitable for the high backs of seat furniture.

The laminate (a precursor of modern plywood) was usually about one inch (2.54cm) thick. It

One of Belter's favourite motifs was an imitation cornucopia, as shown in this side chair of c.1850. The extravagance of Belter's work is typically American, although his carving style tended toward Germanic originals, and in fact many of the designs were carried out by highly skilled German immigrant craftsmen.

MEEKS & SON (American, 1797-1868)

The New York firm of Joseph Meeks & Son was Belter's main competitor. Meeks concentrated on formal pieces in the Federal style of Duncan Phyfe or the American Empire taste. But the company is best-known for its rosewood cabinet furniture in the Neo-gothic style, produced in the 1850s. Some pieces were laminated.

Inlaid, ebonized cherry dressing table by Herter Brothers
c.1880-85; ht 99 -¹/₄in/239.4cm; value code A

Identification checklist for the Aesthetic furniture produced by Herter Brothers
1. Is the piece made principally from cherrywood?
2. Are any surfaces ebonized or do they show rich patination?
3. Is the form rectilinear and relatively simple?
4. Is the design free of applied ornament?
5. Is there extensive inlaid decoration, in a formalized Japanese style?
6. Is any inlay work well executed, intricate and in a variety of materials?
7. Do the inlaid motifs include stylized chrysanthemum leaves?

Herter Brothers (The United States, 1865-1905)
Herter was founded in New York by the half-brothers Gustave and Christian Herter who, like J. H. Belter (see pp.30-31), emigrated to the United States from

Stuttgart in the mid-19thC. While Gustave concentrated on conventional and revivalist designs, Christian produced more adventurous pieces inspired by the English Aesthetic movement, in particular by the designs of

E.W. Godwin and Christopher
Dresser. He was also greatly
influenced by the contemporary
fashion for Japonisme. Gustave's
furniture is of little collectable
interest today, but Christian's fine
Aesthetic designs are highly
desirable.

Gustave returned to Germany in
the 1870s but Christian remained,
and under his directorship Herter
Brothers became the most
progressive furniture design
company in the United States. In
1882, he completed an ambitious
interior for the Vanderbilt
mansion in New York. The
marble and cherrywood dressing
table in the main picture was
made for this scheme. Christian
died a year later and, although the
company continued in production
until 1905, little furniture of
interest seems to have been made
after his death.
* Herter's furniture is rarely
signed but most pieces can be
easily identified by their
characteristic style as well as their
high design and manufacturing
standards.

Custom-made furniture
Many of the firm's commissions
came from wealthy American
families, such as the Vanderbilts,
for whom the brothers provided
high quality furniture, as well as
exotic furnishings which they
imported from France, and the
Near and Far East.

This three-fold screen was
custom-made c.1877, for Mark
Hopkins' mansion at Nob Hill
Residence in San Francisco. It
displays typically Aesthetic
elements, being of ebonized wood
highlighted with parcel gilding.
Examples of such custom-made
designs rarely appear on the
market and are eagerly sought by
museums. Herter pieces were
expensive, and are thus usually
found in excellent condition.

Aesthetic furniture
Herter's Aesthetic furniture is
relatively simple in outline,
following the principles of design
set out in Charles Locke
Eastlake's *Hints on Household Taste*
(see p.21), a book that
undoubtedly influenced Christian
Herter's work. Most pieces are
ebonized, or stained and polished.
Gilding is common, and most
examples are extensively inlaid
with satinwood, mother of pearl,
brass, ebony and ivory.

The typically Aesthetic design on
this pair of pedestals, consisting of
wild flowers and a butterfly, is
created using inlaid maple and
bird's eye maple. Herter often
incorporated florettes of stylized
chrysanthemums (Japan's national
flower).

Anglo-Japanese furniture
Herter Bros. produced Anglo-
Japanese furniture from c.1876.
These pieces are simple and
generally made of ebonized wood
with Oriental designs picked out
in lighter tones with marquetry.

The crestrails of these ebonized
chairs are inlaid with flowers and
bamboo sprigs over a lattice splat.
Anglo-Japanese pieces tend to be
on a small scale and to be made in
cherry, rosewood or dark-grained
hardwoods.

Throughout the 1880s the firm
also produced revivals of Gothic,
Renaissance and Egyptian styles,
as well as some re-creations of late
18thC English pieces.

The Four Ages of Man, *a leaded stained glass window attributed to Heaton, Butler and Bayne, c.1872*

The Victorian period witnessed a revival in Britain of a flagging glass industry, both for decorative and useful wares. Although some glassware continued to be hand-blown, the introduction of mass production techniques had a big impact on the industry – for example, for the first time it was possible to make precision pint pots, using the moulded process. This led to the introduction of glass drinking vessels in taverns, in place of the more expensive (and less hygienic) pewter.

In the early years of Victoria's reign, the well-tried, clear glass shapes of the Georgian period predominated, but embellished with various types of cutting.

In 1845, the repeal of the glass act, which had made English glass expensive to produce, led to a fashion for ornate engraved glassware, much of it inspired by the work of French glasshouses such as Baccarat and Saint Denis.

The importation of mass-produced Bohemian colour-flashed and engraved glassware helped stimulate a demand for coloured glassware, hitherto shunned by most British glassmakers, with the exception of the cobalt blue and green glass tablewares traditionally ascribed to Bristol but by no means produced solely in that area.

English glassmaking was taken to its zenith during the last quarter of the century by the glassworks of Thomas Webb. Webb's superb cameo wares illustrate an exemplary standard of craftsmanship, especially the large exhibition pieces, many of which incorporate multiple layers of colour. Often, several people were responsible for the carving of one piece. At the other end of the scale, the glassworks of northeast England provided inexpensive moulded glass objects, usually of small size, that were often more decorative than useful. The most popular colours were vaseline and a sapphire blue that was sometimes opaque at the edges. Beaded glassware was also popular, especially for commemorative wares. The decoration, which was applied over clear glass, consisted of tiny moulded beads, which gave a jewel-like effect. Some incorporated verses or mottos.

The American market was adequately catered for by the home manufacturers such as Steuben, the Boston & Sandwich Glassworks, and the Mount Washington Glass Company (see pp. 50-1). Pressed glass (see pp.40-1) and moulded forms were preferred to hand-blown wares.

The revival in the Victorian age of church building led to a renewed interest in stained glass, especially among the Arts and Crafts Guildsworkers (see pp. 10-11). The principal makers and designers were Sir Edward Burne-Jones, William Morris, Holliday and Kempe, and Heaton, Butler & Bayne. Unfortunately, stained glass has not survived in quantity, much of it having been discarded in the 1950s and 60s, when religious subjects were not popular with collectors.

Hand-blown glass exhibits either a pontil mark (where the glass has been broken off the rod in the making) or a smooth concave polished surface where the pontil mark has been ground or polished away. Moulded pieces often incorporate either a moulded signature or a registration mark (see pp. 184). When unmarked, they might exhibit mould lines on the exterior or at the footrim and in certain instances might still retain small pieces of flash – excess glass left behind when the object was taken from the mould.

Victorian glass has survived in some quantities. Once spurned by collectors it is now very sought-after and prices have probably increased by 500 percent in the last 15 years. All cameo glass is expensive, especially the larger pieces, and the very desirable cameo glass plaques produced and signed by George Woodall of Webb. By contrast, the market for novelty wares has recently gone into decline.

STOURBRIDGE

A vase made in Stourbridge by Stevens & Williams
c.1890; ht 8 ¹/₄ in/22.5cm; value code F

Identification checklist for Stourbridge novelty glass
1. Is the piece decorative rather than functional?
2. Is it of "fancy" (elaborate and novel) form?
3. Does the decoration include applied flowers, fruit or trailing motifs or feathering?
4. Are any rims crimped?
5. Are any leaves fern-like or veined?
6. Is the item cased (see p. 176)?
7. Does it have a satin or high-gloss surface?
8. Does applied decoration show evidence of pincer work?
9. Are there tonal variations in the main colour?

Stourbridge
The group of factories in Stourbridge in the English Midlands is mainly remembered for the cameo glass by Thomas Webb & Sons (see pp.40-1) and Richardsons, and for the novelty glass produced by several factories, the principal one being Stevens & Williams (later Brierly Royal Crystal). Some, but not all

Stevens & Williams pieces bear a signature, but not all glassmakers signed their work and attribution often has to be made on the strength of subtle differences – for example, in the manner of decoration.
* The wavy edge of the vase in the main picture was so popular in the 1870s that many Stourbridge firms patented their crimping method.

"Fancy" glass

The vase and epergne shown here are typical of the "fancy" glass made from the mid-19thC, when coloured glass in novelty forms came into its own. Such pieces represented a departure from earlier English coloured glass in that they were purely decorative. Some show an Italian influence – the form of the vase was probably inspired by the Murano-based firm, Salviati. Although Stourbridge was the main centre of production in England, fancy glass was also made in the northeast of England, and in London by James Powell. It was also very popular in the United States. Typical novelty features of these wares include:
* the use of toned glass (particularly noticeable in the vase, which varies from white to apple green).
* applied fruits (especially Stevens & Williams) and flowers, either clear or opaque. Fern-type leaves were also used.

Nailsea glassware

The Nailsea glassworks, based near Bristol, England, produced domestic wares in dark brown or green glass. In order to make their wares more attractive, they perfected a method of fusing or splashing on pieces of coloured or white enamel. The process was widely copied.

The decorative effect exemplified by the multicoloured feathering of the ornamental pipe *above* has, in the past, always been associated with the Nailsea glassworks, to the extent that Nailsea is now almost a generic term for this type of fancy glassware. However, it is becoming more apparent that the majority of examples are probably the work of either the Stourbridge factories or of those glassmakers working in the northeast of England. Other items in this style include rolling pins, ornamental shoes and bells, and many types of ornamental vessels, including lozenge-shaped flasks, sometimes with multiple joined flasks and incorporating two spouts. A variety of colours was used.

Spun-glass ornaments

Fancy spun-glass ornaments housed under glass domes, many of them made in the Stourbridge area, are very collectable today. Exotic glass birds were popular but the most sought-after type is that depicting a stuffed bird – usually a hummingbird or canary – within an ornamental glass cage. Ship subjects are also popular and are valued according to their size and the number of "extras" – for example, whether the piece incorporates figures of sailors or a lighthouse, or is "afloat" on a spun glass sea. These ornaments are never marked.

Epergnes

Coloured glass epergnes, or flower stands, were popular during the 1860s. (Previously epergnes had been made only in silver or clear cut glass.) They are invariably ornamental rather than functional.

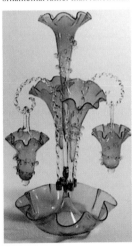

The firm of George Ernest Fox, a few miles from Stourbridge, made a number of epergnes in the late 1890s, including this cranberry example, with its characteristically irregular colours. No two are identical, and many show evidence of hand manufacture. The barley twist bracket supporting the baskets is typical, as is the trailing decoration. The number of vases varies; some examples have as many as five or six radiating from a central trumpet.
* Cranberry-coloured epergnes are more popular than those in other colours.

THOMAS WEBB & SONS

The Dancers, *a Webb cameo plaque ascribed to G. Woodall
c.1880; dia.12 1/2 in/32cm; value code A*

Identification checklist for Webb cameo glass
1. Does the piece feature three-dimensional, cameo-style relief decoration, probably highlighted in white?
2. Are human forms partially visible through diaphanous drapes?
3. Is the decoration inspired by Neo-classical themes, treated in a lively way?
4. Is the piece marked?
5. Is the underlying glass body either bright yellow, plum, blue or brown?
6. Is the surface of the piece silky?

Thomas Webb & Sons (English, 1856-present)
Thomas Webb's glassworks at Stourbridge began producing finest quality wares in 1856. Its reputation was founded on three main types of glass: cameo glass Burmese ware, and rock crystal.

Marks
All Webb cameo glass was etched on the base: "THOMAS WEBB & SONS". Rock crystal wares are stencilled with either "Webb" or, on later pieces, "Webb, England". George Woodall signed most of his pieces "GEO. WOODALL".

Cameo glass
Cameo glass is composed of two or more layers of glass, often of varying colours, carved on a wheel or etched to make a design in relief. Webb's very high quality cameo glass was hand-made under the direction of the firm's main designer, George Woodall. Woodall's own decorative themes tend to be based on Neo-classical subjects, but his lively and subtle treatment avoids the stiltedness usually associated with that style. His almost three-dimensional figures are often partially visible through diaphanous drapes.

Woodall's cameo reliefs were highlighted predominantly in white, as displayed by the rare shouldered vase, *above*, which depicts the goddess Flora as a young girl.

Other decorators at Webb's introduced layers of pale pink and yellow as well as white into their cameo reliefs. The latter effect is visible in this four-colour ovoid vase, a fine and rare piece that was made by Webb's in c.1880.

Note

* The underlying, translucent glass used by Webb's cameo designers was often yellow, plum, blue or brown.
* The value of each piece depends on the overall quality of design, size (larger pieces command higher prices), and how many layers of cameo it has: multiple layers are the most desirable.
* Most of the cameo wares produced by Webb's were purely decorative, with the exception of scent bottles and flasks.

Other cameo glass makers

Other English cameo glass makers of the period included the firm of W. H. B. and J. Richardson. Their chief designer, John Northwood, developed his own technique of cameo cutting. Northwood was also employed by Stevens & Williams, although he later set up his own workshop. He trained George Woodall, and there are similarities in their work.

Burmese ware

Burmese glassware, distinguished by the merging of pink to pale yellow, was one of several types of art glass developed by the Mount Washington Glass Company in the United States (see pp.50-51) Its striking effect, achieved by combining gold and uranium oxides, had the side effect of making pieces radioactive. Popular with Queen Victoria, it was employed by Webb's under the name Queen's Royal Burmese Ware.

The most sought-after pieces are enamelled, often with a floral motif, like that shown *above*. Gilt enamelling is the most desirable. Fakes and copies abound. Genuine wares should bear a circular stencil mark on the base, which should be ground. Also, the surface of Burmese ware is semi-matt – a granular surface indicates a fake.

Rock crystal

The term "rock crystal" is used here to describe a form of engraved lead glass which is cut to simulate the natural facets of real rock crystal. The engraved surface is polished to achieve the desired effect. Coloured glass embedded with artificial leaves and berries was sometimes employed as a surface feature, and later Webb pieces tend to show an Art Nouveau type of floral design. Typical wares included wine glasses and vases, which are more sought-after. At the time rock crystal was the main source of Webb's income but today it is the least popular of Webb's wares.

PRESSED GLASS

A miniature Sowerby vase in gold vitro-porcelain glass
1879; ht 4¹/₄in/10cm; value code H

Identification checklist for Sowerby's vitro-porcelain glass
1. Has the piece a novel and decorative form?
2. Does it exhibit mould lines?
3. Are the motifs crisply executed?
4. Is the surface of the piece glossy?
5. Is the body almost opaque?
6. Does the piece have a trademark of a peacock's head?
7. Has it a Patent Office Registration mark? (See p. 184).

Pressed glass
Press-moulding glass by mechanical means was one of the major achievements of Victorian glass makers. Most of the wares consist of domestic items such as drinking vessels, jugs, bowls, dishes, celery vases, salt cellars, and so on. These are usually made in clear, colourless "flint" glass. Coloured pieces, sometimes known as "slagware", tend to fetch higher prices.

Many of the designs imitated the fashionable and more expensive styles of cut glass. However, pressed glass motifs are regular but less sharp than in cut glass, and the seam lines made by joins in the moulds are often visible.

Pieces can be precisely identified as most carry a maker's mark or a Design Registration mark (see p. 184). The marks are sometimes difficult to see, but can usually be detected by running a finger over the surface of the glass.
* Pressed glass is of uniform thickness with mould lines sometimes visible on the interior.
* Sculptural pieces command a premium.

Lacy glass
This inexpensive form of machine-pressed glass, developed in the United States in the 1830s, is categorized by its intricate patterns. Pieces made before 1840 are in great demand.

Sowerby (English, 1847-1972)

Some of the best quality pressed glass, such as the piece shown in the main picture, was made by Sowerby's Ellison Glassworks in Gateshead on Tyne. They registered their products with the Patent Office from 1872 and introduced their peacock's head trademark in 1876.

The most sought-after glass is made of vitro-porcelain, which looks rather like porcelain or bone china, and was produced from 1877. It was manufactured in a wide range of colours, including cream (when it was called "Patent Ivory Queen's Ware"), white, gold, pale turquoise and jet (appearing black, but usually deep purple). The glass was also available in various marbled colours, such as purple, blue and green (malachite).

The Sowerby range consisted of vases, spill holders and wall pockets, small baskets, candlesticks and other ornamental items, but also ribbon plates and stands for dessert services. The designs were mostly in the 1870s and 1880s "Aesthetic" style, some in imitation of carved ivory and showing a Japanese influence; others derived from children's book illustrations by Walter Crane (1845-1915).

George Davidson (English, founded 1867)

Davidson's Teams Glass Works at Gateshead also produced a wide variety of useful and ornamental wares in clear and coloured glass. Their trademark was a lion above a crown within a circle, or from c.1880-90, a lion above a tower. This glass jug and tumbler was made in their "Pearline" glass, patented in 1889. Coloured blue or primrose, the patterns usually imitated the current fashion for "brilliant" cut glass.

Henry Greener (English, founded 1858)

From the late 1850s, this Sunderland works manufactured good quality clear and coloured glass. Like Davidson's, they produced many items to commemorate Queen Victoria's Jubilee in 1887, as well as other royal and historic occasions. Their

mark was a lion with a star, and after 1885, a lion with an axe. This pressed glass bowl was made to celebrate the Silver Wedding Anniversary of the Prince and Princess of Wales in 1888. The beaded lettering is characteristic of Greener's wares. It was also used by Davidson and copied on the Continent. The Continental pieces, which are unmarked, are of inferior quality.

Henry Greener,
used 1875-85

Greener & Co.
used c.1885-1900

Other makers

In Britain, high quality pressed glass was also made by the Manchester firms of Molineaux, Webb & Co., and John Derbyshire. In the late 1860s and 1870s, both companies issued designs in Greek key patterns, and star and leaf motifs with frosted effects that contrasted with the shiny body. Derbyshire also manufactured lions after the painter Sir Edwin Landseer, as well as figures of Britannia and Punch and Judy.
* The best known maker in the United States was the Boston & Sandwich Glass Company (1825-88), who specialized in the production of lacy glass.
* The most sought-after American pressed glass is commemorative.

CONTINENTAL GLASS

A Bohemian vase commemorating the Great Exhibition at Crystal Palace, London, in 1851
1851; ht 10in/25.5 cm; value code G

Identification checklist for Bohemian engraved glass
1. Does the piece exhibit fine-quality engraving, perhaps of stags and hinds or German spa towns?
2. Is it colour-flashed in ruby or amber? (Purple or amethyst are also found occasionally.)
3. Is the form heavy?
4. Are the foot and neck rim of star or flower section, with cutting to the underside?
5. Is the piece panel-cut?
6. Does the engraving show clear against a frosted ground?
7. If decorated on one side, does the reverse have a prism panel?

Bohemian engraved glass

A large amount of glass was made in Bohemia and Austria during the 19thC. Exports increased after the 1851 exhibition. Wares consisted of vases, liqueur sets, goblets, chandeliers and candelabra.

The most usual engraved subjects are stags in woodland settings, views of named German spas or Rhineland towns, and exhibition buildings. Colour has a bearing on value: ruby is the most sought-after. Signed examples are rarer, and more expensive: desirable names include Dominik Bieman, Andreas Mattoni and Emmanuel Hoffman.

Later, cheaper examples were made of thinner, mould-blown glass showing pontil marks. The engraving of these tends to be weak and the coloured flashing irregular. Other mass production techniques, such as acid-cutting, often resulted in poor definition.

Some Bohemian wares are overlaid, with decorative overlay cutting or with engraved panels, hand-enamelled portrait medallions, or gilding.

French opaline glass

French opaline glass tends to have been used by decorators almost as an alternative medium to porcelain, which it resembles. This type of glass tends to be heavier than its other Continental counterparts, and often exhibits polished and ground pontil marks.

Mary Gregory Glass

Named after a decorator at the Sandwich Glassworks who painted figures of small children on white enamel vases, dressing table sets and so on, Mary Gregory glass was mass-produced in Europe and the United States. Bohemian examples, such as that shown *above*, usually depict older children, often with coloured facial detail. American versions tend to show infants, and to use only white enamel.

Venetian glass

The use of strong, often contrasting colours, typifies the glasswares made in Venice in the 19thC, especially on the island of Murano. Many employ a range of techniques.

Decoration on opaline wares tended towards asymmetrical sprays of flora trailing over highly formalized bands of gilt flower and leaf decoration, as in the example *above*. Bases and footrims are often embellished with gilt bands of arabesques.
* Some opaline glass by Bohemian and lesser French makers is to be avoided. These pieces are light in weight, and often have a moulded base, which may exhibit a pontil mark.

This exuberant chandelier combines enamel, engraving, casing, air-twist and relief-moulded S-brackets. It also shows the pleated and crimped rims which were especially popular in this type of glassware.

PAPERWEIGHTS

A Baccarat blue-and-white carpet ground weight
1848; dia 3in/7.5cm; value code C

Identification checklist for Baccarat silhouette weights
1. Do any animals depicted in the silhouettes include a
dog, deer, horse, monkey, elephant, goat, or squirrel?
2. Do any birds include a stork, cockerel, swan,
pheasant, pelican, pigeon or lovebirds?
3. Are the silhouettes set against an all-over carpet or
muslin ground?
4. If the canes include the initial "B" above the date, is
the date either 1847, 1848, 1849, 1853 or 1858, with the
numerals in red, blue or green on white canes?
5. Do any flowers contain an arrowhead motif?
6. Does the weight have a slightly concave or star-cut base?

Glass paperweights
Paperweights are made by placing
tiny sections cut from coloured
and patterned rods or "canes" in a
mould; these are then set in clear
molten glass. It is possible to
identify a paperweight through an
examination of the motifs used to
decorate the canes and the way
the canes are grouped. Some
weights are signed. Surrounds are
usually smooth. Faceted examples
and those in "overlay", with a
coloured coating partitioning the
surface into separate viewing
areas, are rarer.

Reproductions are usually lighter
in weight than the originals, and
unlike them, tend not to get
narrower toward the base.
   * Check that the motifs are
complete and that pieces have not
come away.

Baccarat (French, founded 1764)
This Alsatian glassworks made
weights between c.1845 and
c.1849. Many of their pieces carry
an initial B and a date marked in
red, green or blue on white canes.
Baccarat produced a large number
of often densely-packed *millefiori*
("thousand flower") weights, such
as that shown in the main picture,
in which the canes are cut to
resemble tiny flower heads, and
are laid on an all-over carpet, or
muslin, ground.

This weight is an example of Baccarat's rare coiled snake motifs. It is mounted on a ground called a *fond filigrane Venise*.
* Avoid weights with large air bubbles around the animal.

Sulphide weights, which are comparatively rare, contain pictorial or portrait medallions made of china clay or glass paste. This mid-19thC Baccarat example has a faceted surround.

St Louis (French, founded 1767)

Baccarat's closest rival produced its finest weights between 1844 and 1850, after which the company virtually ceased making them altogether. A few bear dates between 1845 and 49; the most common date is 1848. The numerals are in blue, purple, mauve or red, often with the initials "SL" in black or blue.

Many St Louis weights depict large single flowerheads: this dahlia is typical.
* St Louis weights have higher domes than Baccarat versions, and usually have star-cut bases.

A poular ground pattern was the *latticinio* design, seen in this St Louis clematis weight, in which threads of opaque, molten glass are woven into a lattice design.

Clichy (French, 1837-75)

The best Clichy weights were made between 1846 and 1852. Clichy weights are spherical with a flat, slightly concave base. Most have a depressed ring near the base where the mould mark has been imperfectly removed. The glass is usually lighter than in Baccarat or St Louis weights. A few examples include an opaque white cane depicting the letter C in black, blue, red or green. Some have the name inscribed in full.

Among the factory's most distinctive designs (although not exclusive to them) is the "Clichy rose", often used as the central motif, as here, with typical looped hooks on an upset muslin ground.

The swirl weight *above* is another typical Clichy style. Clichy weights are regarded by many collectors as the best and tend to command the highest prices.

American weights

Glass weights were introduced to the United States in c.1851. Generally, the designs tend to follow European originals, but many pieces show a distinctive American ingenuity. The most important American factories were the New England Glass Co., the Boston & Sandwich Glass Co. and the Mount Washington Glass Company (see pp.50-1).

This "crown" weight was made by the New England Glass Co. The design always has a pattern of twisting ribbons radiating from a central device.

ENAMELLED GLASS

An enamel, acid-etched and gilded jardinière by Émile Gallé
c.1885/90; dia 12in/31cm; value code B

Identification checklist for enamelled glass by Émile Gallé
1. Is the piece signed?
2. Are the motifs floral and naturalistic, Iznik (see facing page) or of medieval inspiration?
3. Is the decoration applied over a tinted – perhaps green or grey – base?
4. Are mushrooms or insects among any naturalistic motifs?
5. Does the decoration include gilding?
6. Does the base have a ground and polished pontil?

Émile Gallé (French, 1846-1904)

The foremost French glassmaker of the 19th and early 20thC, Gallé established his workshop in Nancy in 1874, producing glass in a wide variety of styles and techniques. The firm made useful and decorative wares, including liqueur sets, decanters, lamps and drinking glasses. The enamelled glasswares belong emphatically to the Victorian period, and represent Gallé's initial foray into the world of the glassmaker. He exhibited work in this medium from 1878, and his earliest designs were mainly influenced by decoration from medieval France.

By the end of the 19thC Gallé preferred more sculptural, naturalistic plant and insect forms. He often incorporated flowers (especially cowparsley) peculiar to the Nancy region of Lorraine, where he grew up. Mushrooms were another recurring theme in his work, often simply as decorative motifs, although some of his lamps imitate the fungus's entire shape.
* The enamelled piece in the main picture is also acid-etched which gives it a texture, and makes it more desirable than pieces that are only enamelled.
* The bases of Gallé's glassware usually have ground and polished pontils.

Value

Enamelled wares are still regarded as the poor cousins of Gallé's later studio productions and are relatively undervalued. Assuming comparable quality, price usually depends on size.

Signatures

All Gallé pieces are signed, but in a variety of ways. The signatures are often found on the base, marked in black enamel or gilt. The gilt may be worn away making it necessary to hold the object in the light to see the trace of the original mark, which is relatively small. Gallé reserved his most elaborate, carved signatures for more important pieces.

* Some of his earlier, historical pieces incorporate the cross of Lorraine in the mark (although this device was also used by other French glassmakers).

Iznik-type (or "Islamic") wares

Iznik-type ware was the term given to ceramics and glass inspired by the brilliantly-coloured pottery produced at Iznik in Turkey in the 15th and 16thC. Typical designs take the form of stylized flowers or arabesques, often with (genuine or fake) Koranic scripts woven into the decoration.

This enamelled glass bowl illustrates Gallé's adaptation of an Iznik, or Islamic, design to a form of Art Nouveau. It is signed "E Gallé Nancy" on the base.

* Human figures never appear on Iznik-type wares, although stylized animals and birds sometimes figure.
* "Iznik" wares fetch higher prices than non-Iznik enamelled glass.
* Gallé learnt many of his techniques from Brocard (see right); Gallé, Brocard and Lobmeyr (below) are considered to be of equal stature, although pieces by Gallé now tend to command higher prices.

Lobmeyr (Austrian, established 1864)

The Viennese firm of Lobmeyr was among the few other European glassmakers to produce high quality Iznik-type wares in the 19thC, although they did not confine themselves to this form of decoration.

This Lobmeyr enamelled and gilded vase, with its characteristically precise decoration, contains an Arabic inscription below the neck of the vase which reads *Ma Shaa' Allah* (The will of Allah) repeated in German, alongside the maker's monogram, on the base.

* The Lobmeyr signature is often inscribed in black enamel.

Phillipe-Joseph Brocard (French, active 1867-90)

Another French maker of enamelled and Iznik-type wares, including lamps, vases and bowls, was Joseph Brocard, who signed his wares "Brocard", sometimes with the address of the firm, or "Brocard et Fils".

This enamelled opalescent glass vase by Brocard, although not wholly Iznik, nevertheless has Persian-style carnations and foliage edged with gilding – characteristics of many Iznik wares. It bears Brocard's signature on the base.

47

JAMES POWELL & SONS

A glass vase by James Powell & Sons
1885-90; ht 8¹/₄in/19.5cm; value code F

Identification checklist for glass by Powell & Sons

1. Is the body of vaseline, or edged in toned vaseline?
2. Is the piece ribbed, fluted or undulating?
3. Does it resemble Venetian glass, or the more informal, irregular and organic shapes of Art Nouveau?
4. Is a decorative feature made of the rim – for example, by crimping?
5. Does the piece look at least partially transparent, light and elegant?
6. Is it hand-blown?
7. Are the pontil marks polished (see p. 35) ?
8. Is the item tableware, a vase or a light fitting?

James Powell (English, 1835-1914)

James Powell was one of the foremost makers of studio glass in the Victorian period. Typical 19thC products include goblets and wine glasses, carafes, decanters, table centrepieces, vases, candelabra and paperweights. Powell preferred light and elegant designs to the heavy forms of Victorian cut glass.
* Few of Powell's designers are known today, with the exception of Phillip Webb and Joseph Leicester, a superlative craftsman whose wares won several

important prizes.

Note

On some of Powell's products, the pontil marks were deliberately left unpolished to suggest age, especially on their reproductions of ancient Roman glass.

Collecting

Some of Powell's exhibition pieces are now extremely valuable, but the simpler wares such as vases and goblets have recently fallen in price and are relatively inexpensive. None of the wares are marked.

CHRISTOPHER DRESSER

The vase shown *above* has several features typical of Powell's vases and drinking glases of c.1885-90:
* slender stem
* wide, flat foot
* fluted rim
* undulating body. (Ribbing was also common.)

Types of Powell glass
* Early 1850s Anglo-Venetian glass, with delicate, gem-like patterns adopted from Venetian models. The decorative techniques were applied onto and inside the glass itself, and included *latticinio* (lattice work), spiral threading in opaque white enamel, beading, and diamond "air trap" designs.
* Early 1850s, "silvered" glass. This involved injecting the metal between two separate layers of glass via the pontil.
* Lead glass reproductions of ancient Roman designs.
* Table glass designed by Philip Webb in 1859, much of it green. It exemplified Arts and Crafts utilitarianism and inspired many glassmakers. Powell's also made some later editions of Webb's range which incorporate lilac stems and beading.
* "Tear-drop" table wares, retailed by Liberty & Co from the late 19thC.
* From c.1889, soda lime glass that exemplified the firm's practical and aesthetic ideals: although light in hand, it is far tougher than it looks.
* Vaseline glass or, as in the main picture, vaseline glass inclusions. This is a type of pale yellow-green, opalescent colouring that thickens and changes colour at the rim. In Powell's glass, the vaseline often thickened to blue. The firm frequently employed this tone when making shades for Benson's light fittings (see p.136). Vaseline glass is also known as yellow opaline.

The other main British producer of art glass was Christopher Dresser (see pp.130-1), who designed this marbled, *solifleur* vase in the mid-1890s as part of his Clutha range of glassware for the Glasgow firm of James Couper & Sons. His pieces are often signed, but should show the maker's seal as well, as fakes and copies abound. This piece has an acid-stamped seal which reads "Clutha, designed by C.D., registered."

The jug illustrated *above* shows some of the typical features of Clutha ware: the austere, irregular shape offset by pink threading and silver foil inclusions, and the slightly bubbled effect. Yellow and amber versions were also made; pink is the most collectable. Pieces with silver foil inclusions and combed, white striations are especially desirable. Not all Clutha wares are marked: this example is not signed, and could be by Dresser or George Walton, who began designing wares for Clutha in 1896.

*A Royal Flemish vase by the Mount Washington Glass Company
c.1885-95; ht 13 ¹/₄ in/33cm; value code C*

Identification checklist for Mount Washington glass
1. Is the form elaborate, with crinkled or ruffled edges?
2. Is the glass multicoloured or shaded?
3. Is the vessel "plated" or composed of at least two layers of glass?
4. Is the exterior decoration skilfully applied?
5. Is the body blown into patterned moulds?
6. Is the surface of high gloss or satin finish?

American art glass
The American art glass industry developed along roughly parallel lines to its English equivalent. By the mid-19thC, glassmakers on both sides of the Atlantic shared an enthusiasm for the innovative techniques and materials used by Venetian craftsmen. American manufacturers were also inspired by ancient glass, and glass from the European Renaissance and the Near East.

The Mount Washington Glass Company (American, 1837-1958)
Like most early American glassworks, Mount Washington was established near Boston. In 1870, its owner, William L. Libbey, moved the firm to New Bedford, Massachusetts. Its manager from 1874 was Frederick S. Shirley, who was closely associated with the American Aesthetic Movement.

Mount Washington's art glass boom followed the exhibition of contemporary glass at the 1876 Centennial show in Philadelphia. By 1880, the works were making a full range of glassware including chandeliers, tableware and paperweights.

American glassmakers relied on English technology which was often supplied by immigrant employees.

In 1894, the business merged with the Pairpoint Manufacturing Co., but the production of art glass, especially Burmese, continued into the 20thC.

This lamp, made c.1885-95, is an example of one of Mount Washington's most successful products, "Burmese" glass, which the firm made under patent from 1885. It was moulded or free-blown into vases, ewers, bowls, candlesticks, perfume bottles, table and boudoir lamps and tablewares. It usually has a matt satin surface and it is often finished with elaborate ornament including figural painting in polychrome and gold enamels.

Popular motifs included fish, flora, American fauna and "Egyptian" imagery. Some Burmese vessels were "diamond quilted" with a moulded cross-hatch design, or blown into "ribbed" or "hobnail" patterns.
* Mount Washington Burmese is among the most highly valued of

all American art glass. Some examples bear printed Burmese labels, and collectors also look for those signed with the designer's name, especially Albert Steffin, the company's Art Director.
* In some cases, the maker reheated the top edge of the vessel a second time, turning it yellow above the pink rim. These pieces are also highly collectable.
* The most widely produced type of shaded glass was "Amberina", developed at the New England Glass Co. by Joseph Locke, an immigrant from England.

HOBBS, BROCKUNIER
(American, 1845-1887)
This Virginian company was the most well known exponent of the Peachblow technique. Peachblow, or Peachbloom, was a shaded glass with a cased, inner layer of opalescent glass which gave the finished ware the appearance of Chinese glazed porcelain.

This "Morgan" vase was one of many made at Hobbs between 1886-91. It is based on a Chinese Kangxi period porcelain vase belonging to the collection of Mary J. Morgan, and is made of Peachblow glass on cast, pale amber stands. Such pieces are extremely collectable, but the stands are often damaged.

CERAMICS

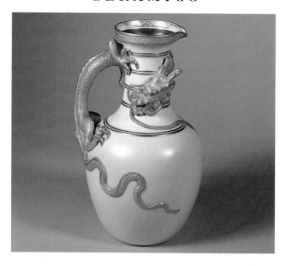

A Copeland Art Union of London stoneware jug, c.1870

The demands of an expanding, increasingly wealthy middle class, and the growing popularity of tea drinking in Britain, led to a huge increase in the Victorian period of tea services and table wares. Hence, in the early years at least, ceramics production concentrated mainly on useful wares in bone china, a newly invented mixture of china clay and ground calcined bone, which was less expensive than porcelain.

The English market for these wares was dominated by firms such as Minton (see pp.72-3) and Coalport (see pp.56-57) who produced copies of the splendid late 18thC French porcelain by factories such as Sèvres. Later in the century, Crown Derby continued to popularize in bone china the colourful Japanese-inspired themes prevalent in all areas of the applied arts during the second half of the 19thC.

In the 1840s and 1850s, the Ironstone china produced by Staffordshire factories, predominantly Masons, was popular until it was superseded by opaque earthenware, which was made largely for domestic use, although the Stafford factories also produced some colourfully enamelled and gilt vases and covers inspired by Chinese ceramics.

The mid-Victorian love of indiscriminate and elaborate decoration was reflected as strongly in ceramics as in any other field. At the Great Exhibition of 1851, even the most humble examples of domestic wares were smothered by beautifully-crafted floral swathes, figures, grotesques and animals. In reaction, pioneers of the Arts and Crafts movement argued for a return to simpler, more practical values in which form and ornament would harmonize, drawing inspiration from shapes in nature and the pre-industrial age. This led, toward the end of the 19thC, to the growth of several small art potteries, who produced an increasing variety of simpler, often hand-made wares.

The influence of the Gothic revival is reflected, amongst others, by Charles Meigh's wares (see p.63). Another peculiarly Victorian vogue was for the simulated cloisonné and Japanese styles produced at Minton's and Worcester.

From the Arts and Crafts Movement emanated the original, organic forms of Sir Edmund Elton, the humorous creations of the Martin Brothers, and the masterly, lustre-decorated wares of William de Morgan.

In the 1880s and 90s, various factories began to mass-produce wares using the technique of slip casting – a diluted, creamy mixture of clay and water cast in moulds that absorb the water. Factories such as Bretby, Burmantofts and Linthorpe produced ranges of slip cast art pottery with unusual glazes, some incise- or *sgrafitto*-decorated, or trailed in the same slip.

The seeds of Art Nouveau can be seen in the Aurelian wares produced in the 1890s by James Macintyre after designs by William Moorcroft, many with Iznik decoration (see p.47).

The new Victorian middle classes also turned their attention to sculpture: unable to house life-size bronzes of their favourite classical, military and political figures, they demanded smaller porcelain copies which could be displayed on a mantelshelf or in a cabinet. Many of these wares were made in "Parian" porcelain (see pp.64-5), a white, semi-matt material that was hugely fashionable during the mid-19thC.

In the United States, 19thC ceramics tended to imitate European models, although some were decorated with specifically American images and emblems, such as bison-head handles, star-spangled banners and American Indians.

Collectors need to be able to identify the "body" or material from which the piece is made and should familiarize themselves with the various types by handling as many pieces as possible. Porcelain has a dense white glassy body. Hard-paste porcelain results in crisp detailed modelling. Soft-paste is similar, but has a softer appearance and is more easily scratched. Pottery is coarser and heavier than porcelain, and has a rougher surface. It is either porous earthenware, which has a granular body, and is glazed, or non-porous stoneware, which has a smoother surface. Unlike porcelain, most earthenware and stoneware is opaque (although some thinly potted earthenware admits light). Most Victorian stonewares are unglazed, although a few pieces are salt-glazed, leaving a pitted surface.

Generally, the hand-made and hand-painted wares of the period are the most desirable, although some valuable wares, including Worcester vases and the figures modelled by James Hadley, depended upon moulded techniques. Moulded wares tend to display mould lines. Identical pieces with precisely matching mould lines will have been mass-produced.

EARLY PORCELAIN

An early Victorian teapot
c.1840-50; ht 9-10in/21.5-24cm; value code F

Identification checklist for early Victorian porcelain wares (c.1837-c.1860)
1. Is the form elaborate?
2. Is the piece bone china?
3. Is any handle extravagantly looped, and moulded with a spur (small protrusion) or several spurs?
4. If a cup, has it a wide mouth and is it mounted on a narrow footrim?
5. Are any finials ornate?
6. If a figure, is it painted in the round (that is, at the back as well as on the front)?
7. Is the piece hand-painted (although some transfer-printed pieces are collectable, see facing page)?
8. If a teapot, is the body ribbed or moulded?

The development of bone china
The most significant development in Victorian ceramics was the transition from 18thC hard- and soft-paste to bone china – a mixture of hard-paste ingredients and large quantities of calcined animal bone. Bone china was especially popular because it was less expensive than previous recipes, and it had its heyday in the Victorian age. Its main features are a soft, translucent body covered by a glassy glaze prone to crazing.

During the early 19thC, porcelain wares tended to echo the Baroque and Rococo fantasies that had evolved when George IV and William IV were on the throne. These shapes provided a ready alternative to the well-tried and somewhat staid classical forms of earlier years. Forms now relied less on silverware than they had previously.
* The bone china wares of some lesser Staffordshire factories were porous. This often led to staining which can be hard to remove.

Teawares

Today, the most sought-after early Victorian teawares were made by the Yorkshire factory of Rockingham, to which a large majority of this type of porcelain is often mistakenly ascribed: identification can be difficult because few pieces actually bear a factory mark. It is therefore essential to gain a knowledge of shapes and the various styles of pattern numbers used by the individual factories. Pattern numbers vary a great deal in style and format, but many are expressed as fractions.

This tea cup and saucer by the Staffordshire firm of Samuel Alcock (established c.1826) illustrates the new shapes that became fashionable in the early Victorian period. The wide-mouthed cup on its narrow footrim and the extravagant loop handle are typical of the period. The spur or protrusion at the base of the handle is typical. Many pieces had several such spurs.

Decoration

Apart from rare pieces such as commemorative items, hand-painted wares are more desirable than those that have been transfer-printed. The teapot in the main picture is decorated by transfer-printing, and embellished with onglaze enamels, but its unusual subject makes it collectable. Wares of this type were sometimes given a pink lustre (a feature often associated with the Sunderland area but not exclusive to it).

Some early Victorian teapots are very inventive, with mythical animal terminals on the spouts and imaginatively treated finials. Typical motifs include seaweed and fronded weeds, and vermicular patterns were also favoured.

* Underglaze cobalt blue tends to have been favoured by many factories, especially Coalport and Minton, but a variety of other colours were used as well.
* Some wares have a pattern number hand-painted on the inside of the footrim.

Figures

Owing to its plasticity, bone china was suitable only for small-scale objects. Production of statuettes was concentrated in the Staffordshire area, and some of the best examples were by Minton (see pp.70-1), whose shepherds and shepherdesses are as exuberant as the classic 18thC figures of Chelsea and Derby. Their wares do not usually carry a Minton mark, but can be identified by their impressed shape number. The same is true of Rockingham wares. Favourite subjects included personalities from literature, and famous people of the day. Many of the figures were made in unpainted, white biscuit (the forerunners of Parian ware, see pp.64-5).
* As in other media, animal figures were extremely popular.

The rare Ridgway and Robey figural group shown *above*, made c.1837, depicts characters from Charles Dickens's popular novel, *Nicholas Nickleby*.
* The Dickens characters are the only known marked pieces produced by the pottery. Unlike the slightly later flatback figures (see pp.58-9), they are painted in the round.

LATER PORCELAIN

A pair of Coalport vases and covers
c.1870-73; ht 17in/43cm; value code D

Identification checklist for Sèvres-style, later Victorian porcelain (c.1860-c.1900)
1. Is the form based on an 18thC original?
2. Are the reserves and body colours typical of the Sèvres factory?
3. Is the piece of fine, white bone china (apparent from the underside, or the interior of a cover)?
4. Is the decoration of Victorian inspiration – for example, is the body opulent and highly jewelled?
5. Is the piece produced to a very high standard?
6. Does the gilding lack finesse and appear flat in comparison with 18thC Sèvres?
7. Does the decoration involve exotic birds, animals or flowers, or depict scantily-clad figures?

Later Victorian porcelain
The Baroque excesses seen in the ceramics at the 1851 Great Exhibition soon gave way to a revival of interest in historical styles. In particular, the opulent porcelains made at Vincennes and Sèvres during Louis XVI's reign found renewed favour with the aristocracy and wealthy middle classes.

The French styles were reproduced by many English firms who had access to originals in public and private collections. The most successful was probably Minton's (see also pp.72-3), who

are said to have used authentic Sèvres moulds which they bought in the 1860s. Minton's wares were of a very high standard, but like most 19thC imitations of the style, the gilding on their pieces is noticeably flatter, more linear and more brassy than the originals.

Minton specialized in replicas of exotic pieces, such as the Sèvres *vase d'éléphants* and the *vaisseau à mat*. Of the many makers competing with Minton, the firm of Coalport was perhaps eventually the more eminent manufacture of ornamental bone china in the later years of the century. Other firms who made reproductions of 18thC French porcelain included Derby, Worcester and Copeland. The Madeley works of Thomas M. Randall redecorated a large number of Sèvres porcelains and decorated many unpainted bodies which they purchased inexpensively from the French factory.

While the typical Sèvres colours of *bleu celeste*, *rose pompadour* and *gros bleu* were still popular, the decoration on many of these wares preempts later Victorian taste, showing a preoccupation with elaborate gilding, exotic birds, animals and flowers, frequently applied to objects with classical shapes.
* Many of the English factories mentioned here also made miniature porcelain for children such as tea services, ornamental vases, coal scuttles and watering cans. The tea wares are often more valuable than the large originals.

This Derby Crown vase and cover, painted in the Sèvres style c.1878-90, echoes the work of the French artist Jean August Dominique Ingres (1780-1867). The combination of gilt relief work and translucent enamel beading was popularized to a state of excess by the premier Victorian French makers.

COALPORT (English, established 1796-present)
This factory's Sèvres-style wares were often embellished with paintings of exotic birds by designer, John Randall. The

Randall piece in the main picture is made of modified bone china, produced by the firm from c.1870 and enabled wares to be made on a larger scale. Apart from birds, figures after the French painter J. A. Watteau also featured on Coalport pieces of this period.
* Some of the earlier wares produced at Coalport are almost identical to Sèvres originals, and sometimes can only be told apart by scrutinizing the porcelain body.
* Wares are often marked "Coalport AD 1750", which signified the date the firm claimed to have been founded, and not of production.
* Coalport artists did not sign their wares until c.1900.

BELLEEK (Irish, 1863-present)
Belleek specialized in openwork baskets applied with finely executed flowerheads. The earliest three-stranded baskets with densely encrusted rims are the finest. They are often simply impressed with a single pad on the underside saying "Belleek". From 1863 to c.1880, wares also carried a printed black mark of a seated Irish wolfhound, harp and round tower. After 1880, "County Fermanagh" and several pad marks were added. From c.1900, the marks changed again. The more pad marks there are, the later the piece was made.

The nautilus shell enjoyed a special popularity, both at Belleek, who made this porcelain vase, and at Royal Worcester and Moore Brothers. Belleek also used shell motifs in their tea wares.

Japan wares
Derby and Davenport continued to produce an interesting range of wares decorated with ornate and colourful Japanese-derived designs in red, cobalt blue and green. The pieces are mostly tablewares and ornamental vases, and often adopt Victorian shapes, along with the traditional classical shapes.

PORTRAIT FIGURES

The Victory, *a Staffordshire portrait figure*
c.1856; ht 12in/30.5cm; value code D

Identification checklist for Staffordshire portrait figures
1. Does the figure have a flat, undecorated back?
2. Is it earthenware (and thus opaque)?
3. Is it hand-painted in onglaze enamels?
4. Does the palette consist of bright, primary colours?
5. Is any facial detail well-executed,?
6. Are cheeks brightly rouged?
7. Is any gilding soft, rather than harsh?
8. Is the base relatively plain, perhaps with a title?

Staffordshire portrait figures
Staffordshire portrait figures
became popular during the early
Victorian period and by 1845 were
being mass-produced on a huge
scale. Most are unmarked; some

can be identified using
contemporary documentation.
Intended for mantelpiece display,
they generally have a flattened
undecorated back, hence they are
often referred to as flatbacks.

Subjects

All the important events and people of the day were popularized in this relatively inexpensive art form. The most collectable of the figures are royal subjects, followed by military figures, and animal (especially equestrian) subjects. There were also theatrical and sporting personalities and murderers, and even the scene of a crime. The Crimean War inspired patriotic figures, often featuring allies or the combined services. *The Victory*, in the main picture, shows England, France and Turkey, three of the parties involved in the Crimean War.

* The most collectable military subjects are those that commemorate the Crimean War.

Scottish figures

Scotland was another important area of manufacture, in particular Glasgow. Scottish figures tend to be slightly heavier than those made in England and make more use of a blue-grey glaze. In addition, they use a distinctive palette that includes claret, pine green, black and ochre.

* Some flatback figures were also made in South Wales.

Early Staffordshire figures

Many of the earliest Staffordshire figures (made in the 1830s and early 40s) were in a bone china or similar porcellaneous material and tended to be decorated in the round. Some of the better figures, such as the example *above*, of Prince Albert, c.1841, were produced by John Lloyd of Shelton and display a good standard of modelling and decoration. Early pieces such as this one tend to be hollow on the underside of the base.

Original, reproduction or fake?

The flatback industry was still going strong in the final years of Victoria's reign and continued into the 20thC, with many of the original Victorian moulds still being used as late as the 1960s. The Victorian originals are identifiable by their crisp moulding, good decorative detailing and attention to facial detail – many women have feathered eyebrows and rouged cheeks. Hair is often combed and stranded to give some detail – not a feature of later reproductions, in which the hair is rendered in a block. Late-Victorian reissues and later reproductions can usually be identified by their scant decoration – for example, several of the Boer war figures are decorated in gilt and white with only the facial detail rendered in colour.

Fakes tend to display exaggerated crazing and often have dirt painted into the crevices. The bases are similarly blackened to suggest age and are usually wiped free of glaze.

Spaniels were popular subjects. Modern copies have blander expressions and duller colours and display fewer signs of attention to detail than the originals. The cushion that supports this example is unusual: flatbacks usually have plainer bases.

* The simple gilt lines, of soft honey-coloured gold, around the base are a typical feature. Figures made after c.1880 tend to use very bright, distinctive gilding, often referred to as liquid gold.

Value

Price is determined by subject matter and rarity. The value of the piece in the main picture, with its desirable, titled, subject matter, bright colours and well-defined modelling and decoration, is worth as much as ten times the value of a more modest example.

STAFFORDSHIRE

A pair of ironstone vases made in the Staffordshire area
c.1835-50; ht 31in/79cm; value code C

Identification checklist for Mason's ironstone (stone china)

(Mason's were the principal manufacturers in the Staffordshire area)
1. Is the piece marked?
2. Is it stoneware?
3. Is it comparatively heavy in weight?
4. Is it covered in a cobalt blue ("mazarin") glaze, combined with gilding or enamels?
5. Does the decoration include chinoiserie, or Japanese designs or motifs?
6. If a vase, is it of comparatively heavy form?

Ironstone

Ironstone began to gain in popularity during the 1820s but reached a peak of popularity in about c.1850. The principal manufacturer was Charles J. Mason, who patented the medium in 1813, although several other firms produced ironstone china wares, among them Spode, Ridgway, Davenport, Folch, H. & R. Daniel and Hicks and Meigh. Most ironstone wares were decorated with chinoiserie or Japanese designs. Vases were of heavy form and again of pseudo-Chinese shape, often with gilt dragons and mythical beast handles and finials. Mazarin blue was a favourite reserve colour, combined with gilt floral and inset coloured enamel decoration.

CHARLES JAMES MASON
(English, 1813-62)
The firm concentrated on large and extensive dinner services decorated in underglaze blue and onglaze enamels with elaborate Imari-type patterns popularized earlier in the century by such manufacturers as Derby, Coalport and Spode.

Marks
The most common early Mason's mark, used 1813-25, shows "Mason's Patent Ironstone China" impressed in a continuous line. During the Victorian period the printed crown and banner was used, with subtle variations on the shape of the crown indicating the date of manufacture. When unmarked, pieces that cannot be definitely attributed to Mason's are simply described as Staffordshire.

In 1862 the firm was taken over by Ashworth's, and became Geo. Ashworth and Brothers. As well as designing new styles, the firm also continued to manufacture the shapes and patterns that had been popular during the 1850 period. These pieces are marked, often with the impressed words "Ashworth Brothers", sometimes within a coat of arms.

Ashworth's also reproduced and adapted some Mason's ironstone designs in earthenware.

Semi-porcelain
Alongside ironstone, another medium for producing very similar wares was the material referred to as opaque china, or semi-porcelain. This is lighter in weight than ironstone, and less sturdy.
* Opaque china was also produced by Minton's, Wedgwood, Ridgway and many others.

This opaque china dinner service was made c.1862-80 by Ashworth and carries the firm's marks and a pattern number. The Oriental-style decoration is typical of the period. (Mythical dolphins were also popular.)

F. & R. PRATT & CO.
(English, 1840-c.1899)
The technique of multi-coloured printing on a white earthenware base was perfected by the firm of F. & R. Pratt & Co., hence the name prattware, although it was made by other firms as well, such as T. J. and J. Mayer, Bates, Elliot & Co. and H. G. and D. Kirkham. Pratt made a variety of wares in this medium, including decorative plates, mugs and loving cups, often with exotic borders and printed to simulate green malachite and seaweed. However, their staple products were their covers for jars intended to contain potted meat, fish paste or "bear's grease" – a gentleman's hairdressing preparation. Although the covers are the focus of interest for collectors, pieces that retain their original jar command a premium. Multi-coloured lids tend to be more desirable than those decorated only in black and white. Subjects include royalty (mostly executed by Jesse Austin), children, bears and fishing and village scenes, like that shown *below*. Some covers are signed on the reverse; many of those printed with Austin's engravings bear his signature.

Glazes
Covers pre-dating 1863 tend to be wiped free of glaze on the edges. Later covers – those that are most commonly found today – have a crazed, bluey-grey glaze.

Reissues and fakes
Reissues are generally marked on the back "F. & R. Pratt & Co.," and carry a statement of reissue from the makers, Royal Cauldon. Fakes tend to exhibit poor-quality printing and weak colours on a heavily crazed base, and are not usually signed.

The cover *above* clearly shows the crazing typical of prattware. The small circle visible halfway down on the right of the cover was used to place the transfer print neatly in position. Not all examples exhibit this feature.

RELIEF-MOULDED JUGS

A large Baggeley relief-moulded jug commemorating the 1855 Paris Exhibition c.1855; ht 15in/38cm; value code D-E (but most are H, see Note)

Identification checklist for relief-moulded jugs
1. Is the jug stoneware?
2. Is it slip cast?
3. Does it have a completely smooth interior?
4. Is the subject historical, biblical or commemorative?
5. If signed, is the signature accompanied by a diamond-shaped registration mark (see p. 184)?

Note

The jug shown on the previous page, with its hand-painted decoration and gilding, is unusually elaborate and will command a premium. Most are without surface decoration.

Relief-moulded jugs

Relief-moulded jugs had been produced during the late 18th and early 19thC, but in a very different style from those made later in the 19thC – often the decoration was applied in a contrasting colour onto a stoneware body to resemble Wedgwood's jasperware.

The explosion of relief-moulded jugs onto the scene during the early Victorian period came about largely as a result of the Registration Act of 1842, which allowed makers to register their designs, thereby preventing other manufacturers from copying them for a period of three years.

Most of the jugs are slip cast in stoneware in various colours, including buff, dark green, pale green, white and grey. Designs were mass-produced, often in graduated sizes and sometimes in sets of three.

As the century progressed, more attention was paid to using the design to complement the form. Relief-moulded jugs continued to be made until the end of the century.

Many of the early Victorian jugs, from the 1840s, were Gothic in

form or decoration, like this *Apostle* jug, *above*, by Charles Meigh, perhaps the best-known and best-selling of all relief-moulded jugs, and still the type most commonly found today.

Biblical episodes were popular. The Jones and Walley jug *below* is entitled *The Good Samaritan*.
* Other popular subjects were

those inspired by novels of the day, especially those of Sir Walter Scott.
* Classical subjects, especially Bacchus, and *putti* with grapes (a favourite with Minton) were in steady demand.

Lids

Some jugs were given Britannia metal mounts and hinged covers (often mistaken for pewter). Covers are weighted so that they lift up when the jug is tilted for pouring. They were made as an optional extra, so many jugs with no cover may nevertheless have two holes into which mounts for a lid could be fixed if required.

Marks

Although there are a number of anonymous jugs, many are marked. The early marks were often impress-stamped against an ornate applied cartouche pad giving the maker's name and location and the date when the design was registered. As the century progressed, most makers impressed their name onto the base and sometimes included the registration mark (see p.184).
* Minton jugs usually have a script "M" hidden somewhere in the cartouche.

Value

Provided that they are in good condition, relief-moulded jugs are among the last items of collectable Victorian wares that can still be bought for modest prices.

PARIAN WARE

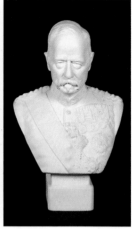

Parian ware busts depicting General Gordon (left) and Lord Roberts (right)
c.1895 and c.1900 respectively; ht of each approx 7in/17cm; value code G/H

Identification checklist for unpainted Parian ware
1. Is the underlying body white or creamy white?
2. Does the piece have a semi-matt surface?
3. Is it a figurine, small portrait bust, piece of tableware or ornamental wall fitting?
4. If a figurine or bust, does it depict a famous personality, a character from classical myth or literature, or an animal?

Parian porcelain
Originally known as "statuary porcelain", Parian (named after the Greek island of Paros, where marble statues were made), was developed as a substitute for the white biscuit figures popularized at Sèvres and elsewhere in the 18thC and early 19thC. The first examples were produced by the English firm of Copeland & Garrett in c.1842-4. Parian is noticeably finer and more highly vitrified than earlier porcelain clays, and it has a slight surface sheen. Statuettes predominate but Parian tablewares and wall fittings also exist.

The medium lends itself to elaborate detail, and several manufacturers took advantage of this quality, notably Samuel Alcock, Minton's, Coalport, Worcester and Belleek.

Surfaces and glazes
While most Parian wares have a white body and semi-matt glaze, some are wholly coloured and others have a high-gloss surface. Some firms used an iridescent glaze to simulate oyster shell. Glazed and unglazed areas could be combined in one piece. Some jugs were glazed inside to aid washing and general hygiene.

Robinson & Leadbeater (English, 1856-1924)
This Staffordshire firm produced some very good examples of Parian ware. Some of their figures were covered in a wash glaze to simulate ivory, but most have matt surfaces. Pieces from the Victorian period are marked with an "RL" surrounded by an oval border, as are the busts in the main picture. The word "Ltd" was added in 1905.

Note
The presence of a brass thread and nut does not indicate a repair: the plinths of some Parian figures were made separately and then joined.

Portraits and sculptures
As in other media, portraits of famous royal, military or political figures were extremely popular. Many of the figures were based on maquettes by well-known contemporary animaliers and sculptors, such as John Bell and Raffaelle Monti. Bell's figure of Dorothea from *Don Quixote* was especially popular, as were Monti's partially-clad or veiled maidens.
* Bell's work often has a pad mark and should not be confused with the Parian ware by John and Matthew Bell of Glasgow, whose products were made from the 1840s, and are marked "JB" with a bell outline.

This delicate figure of a *Water carrier* by Worcester (see pp.66-7) shows the two most common features of Parian porcelain: a smooth, matt surface and a white body, although here the statuette is highlighted in gilt. The subjects were often based on characters from literature, especially Shakespeare's plays.
* Worcester also made very ornate Parian tableware incorporating three-dimensional figures and groups.

Risqué figures such this one depicting a semi-naked woman were often made by Minton. The cream of the drapery is characteristic of Minton's restrained colour scheme. The firm also made finely-detailed Parian tableware and wall-brackets.

Other Parian makers
* Wedgwood
* The United States Pottery Co. at Bennington, Vermont. This firm led the field in the United States, borrowing some of Wedgwood's jasperware patterns before diversifying to include famous events in American history.
* Unnamed Continental firms, notably in France, Bohemia and Thuringia; in the late 19thC they made mostly painted and gilded figurines.

Collecting
As it could be easily mass-produced, the quality of Parian objects varied enormously. Some of the unmarked pieces are of little value, and those decorated with armorial designs and made by Goss in the late 19thC form a separate collectors' market. Size and composition are important factors in determining value, the larger figures being more sought-after.

WORCESTER

A Royal Worcester reticulated vase and cover
c.1890; ht 12in/30.5cm; value code B

Identification checklist for the wares designed by George Owen for Worcester Royal Porcelain
1. Is the porcelain of an ivory-toned colour?
2. Is the piece signed?
3. Is it reticulated (that is, showing intricate pierced decoration), with a variety of patterns?
4. Is the form inventive?
5. Does the palette favour soft colours, particularly duck egg blue and rose pink?
6. Is any decoration highlighted with a soft gilding?

Worcester Royal Porcelain Company (English, 1783-1902)
The original company, Chamberlain & Co. was established in 1783 by Robert Chamberlain. In 1852, it revived under the direction of Kerr and

Binns (the name by which it became known) and under the influence of this "renaissance" became the Worcester Royal Porcelain Company in 1862, producing a wide variety of fine porcelain wares as well as their staple tablewares. The quality of the porcelain is generally excellent, and was never sacrificed for the sake of increased output.

Designers of the Victorian period included James Hadley and Thomas Bott, whose dramatic wares in the manner of 16th and 17thC Limoges enamels, are now extremely rare.

As the century progressed, the wares produced by the company reflected the changes in popular taste. The Aesthetic Movement inspired majolica wares and Japanese-type pieces. These, produced in a blush ivory porcelain and often incorporating hand-coloured enamels on transfer-printed outlines, were the staple products of the late Victorian period. These have survived in some quantity and in good condition.

George Owen's reticulated wares surface in small quantities at most of the London and good provincial auction houses, and in the United States. Demand for all Victorian Worcester is high.

George Owen (British, died 1917)

George Owen specialized in the production of reticulated or pierced wares for the Worcester Royal Porcelain Company during the latter half of the 19thC. His pieces are solely decorative and display an amazing combination of ornate form and dexterity of execution, evident in the vase and cover in the main picture. The porcelain is usually ivory-coloured and applied with elaborate pierced openwork. (This was not innovative: in earlier years Worcester had produced a series of cups and saucers displaying pierced decoration and enamelling.) Decoration tends to be a combination of enamelling and painted, using a predominantly soft palette. The pale blue, pink and pale green of this vase are all characteristic; turquoise is also favoured. Soft gilding is typically used to highlight decoration and is applied to rims, bases, handles and often the main body of pieces. Owen was one of the few designers allowed by Worcester to sign their wares. Most of his pieces have "G. Owen" incised into the clay along with the Worcester stamp – a crowned circle, either impressed or printed. Some exhibition pieces are marked in gilt.

Figural wares, particularly those modelled by James Hadley, proved more popular than any of the sculptural pieces. They are usually functional, incorporating a vase, a bowl or a candlestick. Figures inspired by the drawings of children by the English illustrator Kate Greenaway were the most popular, both then and now. The candlesticks *above* show the late-Georgian dress typical of these figures. Other subjects were inspired variously by Japan, India and Classical Greece; humorous pieces, such as nuns, monks and owls with nightcaps were also popular.

The popularity of Persian-type Iznik wares during the 1880s (see p. 47), inspired a range of vases like that *above*. Those produced by Worcester, like this example, attempted to simulate the precious jewelling of the original Moghul vases, using colourful enamels. The form of this piece, with its slender neck and flange handles, is also typically Persian.

MAJOLICA

A majolica camel by George Jones
c.1880; ht 12in/30.5cm; value code D

Identification checklist for the majolica of George Jones
1. If marked, does the piece carry the impressed monogram "GJ" or does the underside have a rectangular glaze-free area painted with decorators' numerals?
2. Does the inner surface have a mauve/pink glaze?
3. Is the item buff pottery or dark brown stoneware?
4. Is it multi-coloured?
5. Is the decoration hand-painted?
6. Is the glaze slightly uneven?
7. Does the underside display a brown and green tortoiseshell-effect glaze?

Majolica
Victorian majolica was a type of earthenware painted to resemble the colourful glazes of 16thC Italian *maiolica*. Wares are moulded in high relief with a palette of ochres, browns, whites, turquoises, pinks and greens. The term also denotes buff-coloured earthenware decorated in relief under translucent, coloured glazes. Minton dominated the market (see pp. 72-3), but the wares of smaller companies offer a reasonable alternative and are generally less costly.

George Jones (English, died 1893)
George Jones worked at the Minton factory before founding the Trent Pottery in Staffordshire in 1861. As well as white and transfer-printed earthenware made for domestic use, he manufactured majolica and the closely-related "Palissy" ware (also moulded in high relief) from c.1867. Although the Trent firm concentrated on tablewares, it also produced figural pieces and bird and animal statuettes. The animal subjects are very sought-after.

The camel in the main picture is well-modelled and has clearly defined colour areas, which contributes to its desirability. Another version was made in brown stoneware. It is impressed with the title "Kumassie", the letters of the name forming a circle within a round panel.
* Jones's marks were usually an impressed or printed "GJ" monogram. Wares marked with a crescent bearing "& SONS" date from 1873 or later. "England" was added in 1891.
* The colours of those majolica wares by Jones with green and brown glazes tend to be less controlled and more runny than those of other factories.

Brown-Westhead, Moore and Co. (British, 1858-1904)
This pottery produced figural and ornamental majolica wares in a very similar style to those made by George Jones. In 1878, they exhibited a number of majolica vases and plaques at the Paris Universal Exhibition, and they were also noted for their flower-holders decorated with animals.

The Brown-Westhead tiger statuette *above*, c.1878, was made as an exhibition piece and as such can be expected to fetch considerably more than the smaller majolica wares of good quality.
* Ornamental groups by Brown-Westhead are usually impressed with the maker's full name or the initials "B.W.M" within a shield, while the firm's tablewares usually have a printed mark.

Majolica tablewares
Majolica tablewares were made in greater numbers than the decorative animals, and include moulded jugs in the shape of animals or fish, vases and dessert services, fruit bowls, salad dishes, tureens and coffee pots. Those moulded with Japanese-type decoration – for example, those that include fan-shaped panels or depict small birds in flight moulded in low relief – are among the more sought-after pieces.

Wedgwood also produced a range of majolica wares, the most popular of which were oval game dishes ornamented with dead game animals in relief moulding and coloured in cobalt blue, mustard and leaf green. Versions exist in buff earthenware but these are less desirable and at present are worth no more than half the value of their majolica counterparts.
* All Wedgwood majolica is marked.

This Egyptian-style garden seat, c.1870, is of exceptional quality, which makes the lack of a maker's mark all the more surprising. Garden and conservatory furniture was often made in majolica in the Victorian period, and seats based on Chinese originals were especially popular.

Other makers
On the Continent, French and German makers such as Sarreguemines and the Berlin State Porcelain Factory were the most prolific. Rorstrand and Gustavberg manufactured majolica in Sweden as did Cantagalli and Doccia in Italy. Most pieces are unmarked (with the notable exception of Sarreguemines). A number of lesser Staffordshire factories produced moulded tablewares, often with novelty forms. As with their Continental counterparts, the glazes of these pieces tend to be more anaemic than those of the better factories, and wares are unmarked.
Majolica was also produced in the United States by Edwin Bennett and, most notably, by Griffen, Smith & Hill of Phoenixville, Pennsylvania (see pp.92-3).

MINTON MAJOLICA

A massive Minton & Co. majolica urn
1865; dia 33in/84cm; value code A/B

Identification checklist for Minton majolica
1. Is the decoration hand-painted, possibly with figural elements, and in high relief?
2. Are figures slip cast (see p. 53) and therefore hollow?
3. Is the piece marked?
4. Is the body pottery?
5. Is the piece comparatively large?
6. Is it of inventive form?
7. Do even highly decorative wares have a function?
For majolica wares by other firms, see pp.68-9

Minton & Co. (British, 1793-present)
This Staffordshire pottery was established as Mintons, Ltd, and traded under the name Minton & Co. from 1845 until 1873, when it used the name Mintons Ltd. The firm made high-quality earthenware and porcelain. These two pages look at their majolica wares. Minton art pottery is discussed on pp.72-3.
The earliest Minton majolica

dates from the early 1860s and incorporates strong sculptural elements, borrowing from classical, Renaissance and later, Japanese decorative elements. All Minton majolica employs high and full relief decoration. Vases and massive urns tend to be supported upon the shoulders of chubby *putti*, and handles are often embellished with lions' or rams' heads. Most pieces are on a large scale.

Most Minton majolica is figural. One of the foremost modellers commissioned by the firm was the Frenchman Albert-Ernest Carrier de Belleuse who designed these male and female blackamoors, dated 1870, to decorate a pair of candelabra.

From 1870, Minton introduced majolica wares with a strong Japanese influence, such as this dazed-looking ape supporting a garden seat.
* All Minton figures are hollow. The bodies were slip cast separately before being joined together. With so much projecting detail, the figures are extremely vulnerable, and a certain amount of sympathetic restoration is considered quite acceptable.

Marks

Everything produced by the firm is marked "Minton"; objects also have shape and pattern numbers and date codes. Individual years have special symbols (see *right*). There are no fakes or copies.

1842	1843	1844	1845	1846
✳	△	▢	✕	⬭
1847	1848	1849	1850	1851
◠	—	⋈	⌣	∴
1852	1853	1854	1855	1856
⌵	⌂	ↄ	※	♀
1857	1858	1859	1860	1861
◇	⌐	⚦	♌	人
1862	1863	1864	1865	1866
⚸	⬦	Ƶ	≋	⋎
1867	1868	1869	1870	1871
⋊	Ⴌ	⊙	Ⓜ	ℕ
1872	1873	1874	1875	1876
⊗	✕	↓	ℰ	○
1877	1878	1879	1880	1881
◍	△	△	⚠	⊞
1882	1883	1884	1885	1886
⊗	⊘	⊠	⋈	B
1887	1888	1889	1890	1891
⚏	∞	S	T	Ⓤ
1892	1893	1894	1895	1896
⛉	⛊	⛋	⚘	⚘
1897	1898	1899	1900	1901
⚘	⚘	⚘	⚘	①

Minton marks

With its heavily sculpted appearance and figural decoration, this moulded plate depicting Venus is typical of Minton's majolica tablewares. Such an object would probably have been regarded as decorative rather than functional. Other examples are ornamented with portrait medallions suspended from ribbon-tied swags of various fruits and flora. Some of the useful wares made by the firm include tea services, novelty teapots and covered game pie dishes, all with a pottery body.

MINTON ART POTTERY

A Minton & Co. Kensington Studio circular plaque
c.1872; dia 22 3/4in/58cm; value code C

Identification checklist for Minton art pottery
1. Is the detailing and draftsmanship of very high quality?
2. Is the piece marked?
3. Does the decoration include Gothic motifs combined with Oriental or classical figures, or Neo-Renaissance figures?
4. Are small, naked or partially-clad children featured in the decoration?
5. Is the body cream earthenware?
6. Is there much applied or relief detail?
7. Does the decoration look as though it has been built up in layers and hand-carved?
For Minton majolica, see pp. 70-71.

Art pottery

Minton opened a studio at Kensington Gore in c.1870 specifically for producing art pottery which survived for only three years before being burned down. W. S. Coleman, who painted the plaque *above*, was the foremost artist involved with the studio and his work frequently incorporates small naked or partially-clad children, often in classical settings and recognizable by their flat bottoms. He also depicted fantastic or mythological worlds. His draftsmanship and balance of composition is always first class. Most of his work is painted in a typical palette using vivid enamels, but with subtle flesh tones. The pieces bear a printed circular mark for Minton's Art Pottery Studio, Kensington Gore.

Henry Stacy Marks

A leading Kensington Gore studio designer was Henry Stacy Marks, R.A. His *Seven Ages of Man* designs, depicting stylized medieval-type figures in gardens or interiors, were mass-produced by the firm as a series of rectangular ceramic tiles and plaques and were hand-painted in enamels, with gilt highlights. Although the series is virtually impossible to find intact, individual pieces turn up at auction. These are signed "H. S. Marks" and impressed "Minton", and also bear the date code (see p.71), the Studio mark and decorators' monograms. Some bear a paper label giving the title.

Minton Sèvres-style wares

Earlier Victorian products of the Minton factory were made to reflect tastes of that period. Consequently, the craze for French Louis XIV and later 18thC pottery and porcelain resulted in Minton's producing large quantities of Sèvres-style porcelain. This was often so accurate in its rendition that it even confuses experts today.

pieces by Charles Toft in the manner of the French St Porchaire pottery. The candlesticks evoke the Henri II period, although here the Gothic elements (the windows moulded and pierced into the stems) form only a part of the overall decoration which includes Neo-Renaissance figures and Chinese-faced terms as well. The body is cream earthenware.
* Minton produced Gothic wares by other designers such as Pugin.

Pâte-sur-pâte

This method of decoration became popular at Minton through the influence of Sèvres artist and designer, Marc Louis Solon. The technique is painstaking: decoration is built-up and fired in layer upon layer, with hand-carving occurring in between firings in order to achieve depth of tone.
The drawing and craftsmanship of this category of wares were extraordinarily accurate, as seen in

Minton made use of all the typical Sèvres palettes, which included *bleu celeste* and *rose pompadour*, and produced extensive tea and dinner services in these styles. This pair of Sèvres-style vases is decorated in *bleu celeste*.

Minton Gothic

Minton also produced wares in the Gothic style, exemplified by this rare candlestick, one of a pair, made c.1873, and part of a range of

this group of three vases by Solon, c.1875-90. Every piece is unique.
* Price is governed by size: larger pieces are more expensive.
Minton also produced pâte-sur-pâte panels and dessert services. Background reserves include black, dark green, dark brown, terracotta and slate blue.

WILLIAM DE MORGAN

A William de Morgan "Iznik" vase painted by Charles Passenger c.1900; ht 8¹/₂ in/22cm; value code C

Identification checklist for de Morgan pottery
1. Is the piece decorated in lustre colours or a "Persian" palette in enamels?
2. Is it marked?
3. Is it hand-painted?
4. Does it have all-over decoration?
5. If lustre-decorated, is the lustre wholly or partly ruby-coloured?
6. Is any lustre well-controlled and well-executed?
7. Is the piece pottery?
8. Are the bases of plates and chargers decorated on the reverse with concentric bands?
9. Do motifs include fish, stylized flora, birds or animal subjects including grotesques, or single-masted galleons?

The William de Morgan Pottery (English, 1872-1907)
William Frend De Morgan (1839-1917) was the most significant potter to be connected with the English Arts and Crafts Movement. Most of his designs were carried out by others and he worked in collaboration with a number of different artists throughout his life. He is best known for his decorative tiles, but he also created numerous chargers, plates, dishes and vases.

Phases of production
There were three main phases of production:
1. Chelsea phase: 1872-82
Initially, de Morgan bought earthenware blanks of tiles, dishes and vases from Staffordshire and decorated them himself, often in a single-colour lustre glaze. After 1875, he introduced Persian colours, notably vivid blues and greens. Chelsea-period wares tend to be the least collectable.
2. Merton Abbey phase: 1882-87

The repertoire expanded to include dishes, vases, bowls, bottles, jugs and flowerpots, many with elaborate decoration, often enamelled.

3. Fulham phase: 1888-1907
From 1888 until 1898, de Morgan worked in partnership with Halsey Ricardo at the Sands End Pottery in the London suburb of Fulham. He then joined forces with the potters Frank Iles and Charles and Fred Passenger, collaborating with them until c.1905. Most pieces found today belong to this period, which was also responsible for the Persian and Iznik-type wares, such as that shown in the main picture. Many Fulham-period pieces show a greater integration of form and decoration than those from earlier periods.
* While in Florence in 1892, de Morgan employed Italian painters to carry out his designs, and some of the lustre wares produced by the Florentine firm of Cantagalli closely resemble his own.

Motifs
Favourite enamels include all-over patterns of fish, stylized flora, birds, animals and grotesques. De Morgan also favoured single-masted galleons, introduced in the Merton Abbey period.

At Chelsea and Merton, de Morgan tended to concentrate on ruby lustres, and his first two-colour lustre wares date from the Merton period. In these, ruby usually forms one of the two colours. The charger *above*, with a shallow well and wide rim, is painted in amber and puce lustre.

Tiles
Decorative tiles were a staple product of the de Morgan pottery, and were made either singly, to be used in conjuction with others to give a carpet effect, or in friezes or

panels, usually for specific architectural commissions.
* Full panels are very rare, but all the tiles are collectable singly.

Most designs borrow heavily from Persian and Iznik originals, with a particular emphasis on stylized trees, plants and flowers, such as those shown in the detail *above* from an extensive series of tile panels.
* Tiles decorated with ruby lustre glazes and small animals, birds or grotesques are particularly sought-after today.
* Several other large English companies produced decorative tiles, including Maw & Co, who also manufactured de Morgan's tiles, Minton, Wedgwood and Doulton.

Marks
Apart from the ready-made blanks bought from Staffordshire at the start of his career, all de Morgan's decorative and tablewares are signed. He used several different marks or stamps including "Merton Abbey" or "Sands End Pottery" for the Fulham phase, and "DM" or "W. De Morgan". Some marks also include the last two digits of the date in a circle. From c.1880 pieces also incorporate the initials of the decorators, among whom were: Jim Hersey, Joe and M. Juster, Halsey Ricardo, Frank Iles, Charles and Fred Passenger. Tiles are usually marked, but not always with de Morgan's name or initials. Some may be impressed "Carter", the firm who provided the blanks for painting. Others bear the de Morgan flame mark or a circular mark (see p. 179).

DOULTON & CO.

A vase by Florence Barlow for Doulton & Co.
c.1885; ht 14in/35.5cm; value code F

Identification checklist for Doulton & Co. ceramics
1. Is the ground buff or grey stoneware?
2. Does it employ *sgrafitto* (incised) decoration, either applied directly to the ground, or over a coloured slip?
3. Is the piece signed?
4. Does it have all-over decoration?
5. Is the palette relatively subdued?
6. Is the piece hand-thrown and hand-decorated?
7. Is it banded with stylized leaves or flowerheads?

Doulton & Co. (English, 1815-present)
The firm was founded in the early 19thC to produce stoneglaze sewage pipes and sanitary wares. However, in 1871 Henry Doulton opened a studio at his Lambeth Pottery, eventually employing many of the lady artists from the nearby Lambeth Art School. Several of the artists and modellers became pre-eminent in their field, especially the Barlow sisters – Hannah, Florence and Lucy, together with their brother Arthur – as well as George Tinworth, Frank Butler, Mark V. Marshall and Eliza Simmance. The Pottery concentrated on ornamental wares, especially vases and jugs. Most of the artists worked in sombre colours, such as dark green, brown, blue and grey, although the decoration was often lively, spirited and inventive.

Florence Barlow
Florence's wares are typified by the use of *sgrafitto* decoration over a coloured slip, and a preference for small English birds, both features of the piece shown in the main picture. The border around the design is typically elaborate.

Hannah Barlow

Even more than Florence, Hannah used *sgrafitto*. Many of her designs were executed or completed by junior assistants. Her earlier incise-decoration tends to be quite bold in its execution, with scant attention paid to background. However, following an accident in 1876 which left her without the use of her right hand, her work, curiously, became more detailed.

Hannah frequently depicted animals, often sandwiched between elaborate borders, as in this vase, which is typical of her work after the injury. The decoration has been applied over a coloured slip; on earlier pieces it was often incised straight into a buff or grey coloured stoneware, the incise often heightened in dark cobalt blue.

Marks

Most pieces have a number of marks: the artist's monogram, the initials of any assistant, the factory mark, which includes the date, and the marks of other craftsmen who contributed to the piece.

Slater's Patent

This was a technique by which a fabric was pressed into the clay of the leather-soft body before it had completely dried out. When removed, it left an irregular surface which was often decorated with onglaze coloured enamels and overall bright gilding.

Doulton at Burslem

In 1883 Doulton set up another factory in Burslem, Staffordshire, to produce earthenware table and toilet wares, such as jugs and basins. These wares, which tend not to be as sought-after as the Lambeth pieces (although bone china produced at Burslem is more sought-after), include the word Burslem in the mark.

George Tinworth

The work of this outstanding modeller included architectural commissions, especially large multiple figural tableaux. He is also known for his endearing small models of mice and frogs, often in humorous situations and accompanied by incised titles.

Tinworth also decorated ornamental wares. This stoneware tankard is typical. He was the only Doulton artist allowed to put his monogram on the piece itself (rather than on the underside).
* The jug has been repaired, having been broken into several pieces. It lent itself well to restoration because it was possible to simulate the irregular glaze. Nevertheless the value will be reduced by 50-60 percent. Even a chip can cause a drop of 30-50 percent.

Doulton faience

This group of wares is notable for its well-executed decoration, which consists largely of English flowers against toned reserves, often ochre toning to yellow-green or green toning to pale blue.

Faience with figural decoration is scarce and consequently desirable, especially if children are the subjects, as they are in this pair of moon flasks.
* These wares are currently undervalued and prices are bound to rise.

THE TORQUAY POTTERIES

A Watcombe pilgrim flask, decorated after a design by Alexander Fisher c.1881; ht 12in/30.5cm; value code F

Identification checklist for Torquay pottery
1. Is the piece terracotta?
2. Is it marked by one of the known Torquay factories?
3. If the piece is glazed, is the glaze turquoise?
4. Does any floral decoration consist of large flowerhead and leaf designs?
5. On enamelled pieces, does the decoration include small birds, or flowers, perhaps of the English wayside?
6. Is the piece figural or does it contain figural or floral decoration?
7. Is it decorated with slip glazes?

The Torquay potteries
Torquay pottery is the name given to the wares produced by a number of ceramics firms based in and around Torquay in Devonshire, England. The most prolific of these were the Torquay Terracotta Company, the Watcombe Terracotta Company and the Aller Vale Potteries. In 1901, Aller Vale merged with Watcombe to become the Royal Aller Vale and Watcombe Pottery Company. All the potteries used the local red clay that lent itself as an ideal medium for the manufacture of both decorative and useful terracotta wares, which enjoyed a revival during the mid- and late Victorian period. Generally, wares tend to be fairly unadventurous in design.

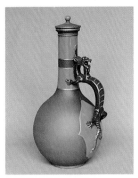

Among the figural terracotta wares are a number of highly detailed groups, such as *You Dirty Boy, below*, modelled by Giovanni

Among the most striking of the Torquay wares are those pieces that contain a turquoise glaze, known as *celeste*, often applied in geometrical bands or motifs to the plain terracotta body, as in this elegant water bottle with a dragon handle. Produced by Watcombe in the late 1870s, its design has been attributed to Christopher Dresser (see p.81).
* Moon flasks and similar items were often made with circular underdishes or stands.

Focardi. The piece was based on a painting used in the campaign to advertise Pears soap. This group was produced by both the Torquay Terracotta and the Watcombe Companies.
* Most of the terracotta statuettes were made in sections and then joined, rather than being made in one piece.

Collecting
The most desirable pieces are the sculptural groups and large, slip-decorated vases. Least collectable are the small souvenirs, motto wares and nick-nacks that dominated the market towards the end of the 19thC and in the early 20thC. Also, avoid painted terracotta wares that are unmarked and on which the decoration appears unprofessional: these were painted by amateurs using terracotta blanks.

Marks
A variety of marks was used.
* Aller Vale impressed their wares with the name of the pottery in capital letters. In the late Victorian period they also used a hand-written incised signature.
* Among the marks used by the Torquay Terracotta Company are the initials "T.T.C." or the name in full, usually surrounding an oval or circle.
* A common Watcombe mark is the printed one shown *below*.

The staple Torquay diet consisted of pieces decorated with coloured slip representing floral studies and small birds in bold designs that exhibit wide brushstrokes, as in the urn *above*, made by Watcombe c.1900. (Compare this with the finer detail of the pilgrim flask on p. 78.) Typically for slip-decorated wares, especially those by Watcombe, the shape is of classical inspiration.
* The slip technique was used to produce the enormous number of motto wares for which the Torquay area is best known.

*A Linthorpe goat's-head vase designed by Christopher Dresser
c.1880; ht 11in/28cm; value code E.*

Identification checklist for Linthorpe and Ault designs
by Christopher Dresser
1. Are the shape and decoration reminiscent of ancient
pottery, such as Celtic, pre-Columbian, Egyptian, or
Islamic, or do they reveal a Japanese or Oriental
influence?
2. Is the piece impress-marked?
3. Does the form utilize simplified or abstract parts of an
animal or plant?
4. Does the glaze appear to have been poured onto the
surface by hand, leaving irregular drip marks, or does it
look speckled or mottled?
5. If Linthorpe ware, are the glazes dark brown with
green, or solid yellow, blue or green?
6. If Ault ware, does it have a spangled glaze?

**Linthorpe (English, 1879-
1882)**
The Linthorpe pottery near
Middlesbrough, North Yorkshire,
was the successful but shortlived
brainchild of noted designer

and aesthete, Christopher
Dresser, and a local landowner:
an artist, Henry Tooth, became
the company's manager while
Dresser was responsible for
creating ideas for new wares.

Today, Dresser's ceramics are among the most highly sought-after of any by a 19thC English designer.

Dresser shared the Arts and Crafts Movement's belief that household objects should above all be functional, but he also had a mystical view of nature, and he brought both attitudes to bear on the pottery he designed for Linthorpe.

Dresser also adapted many of his designs from Celtic, Egyptian, ancient Greek and Roman, Islamic, pre-Columbian and Aztec originals. Later pieces were often painted in slip or underglaze colours, *sgraffito* or slip. Apart from vases, plaques and jugs, the firm also produced salad bowls, cups, and dinner and tea services, all made using clay local to the factory.

The company closed when Tooth set up the Bretby Art Pottery with William Ault in 1882 (see p.82).

Other inventive Dresser shapes for Linthorpe

Glaze effects

Early Linthorpe pottery is noted for its glazes, which Tooth developed in two or more rich colours. Unlike anything seen in Europe before, his slips combined various metal oxides that resulted in irregular flowing, swirling and dripping effects. Dresser's glazes tended to be dark brown with green, or solid yellow, blue or green. The dripping effect of the glaze of the piece in the main picture is typical of his work (as is the use of grotesque shapes, in this case a goat's head).

Dresser's designs, whether simple or complex, were always inventive. Many forms suggest plants or animals: this vase he designed for Linthorpe has an amusing camel-back form.

Ault (English, 1887-1923

William Ault worked in Staffordshire before joining Henry Tooth at Bretby (see p.82). In 1887, he opened an art pottery under his own name at Swadlincote, Derbyshire. He produced ornamental earthenware such as vases, jardinières, pedestals and jugs, as well as objects for domestic use. His daughter, Clarissa, often painted butterflies and plants on his vases.

Many of Dresser's designs for the firm continued the Japanese, pre-Columbian and sensuous, biomorphic themes he had begun while at Linthorpe. The vase *above* has an onion-shaped cylindrical neck and a characteristic turquoise and brown streaked glaze. Dresser also designed some completely new forms, including a series of "egg vases," advertised in 1898. His pieces were also sometimes coated with the shimmering, aventurine glazes invented by Ault.

Marks

Linthorpe ware is marked with the pottery name, sometimes shown over an impressed outline of a squat vase. An incised facsimile of Dresser's signature also appears on some of the firm's pieces alongside Tooth's monogram. The Ault pottery mark is a tall fluted vase over "AULT" on a ribbon or an "APL" monogram. Some of Dresser's pieces are signed as well.

BRETBY ART POTTERY

A pair of Bretby vases
c.1890; ht 12 in/30.50cm; value code F

Identification checklist for Bretby art pottery
1. Are any animals, birds and other figural subjects anatomically correct?
2. Is the piece marked?
3. Is the piece covered with a dark green, amber or ochre glaze?
4. Does the glaze simulate a copper surface?
5. Is the piece earthenware?
6. Is the form relatively simple?
7. Is there a humorous element to the design?
8. Are pairs related but not necessarily identical?

Bretby Art Pottery (English, 1883-1920)
Established by Henry Tooth (who had previously managed the Linthorpe Pottery, see p.80) and William Ault in Derbyshire, Bretby produced mainly earthenware pieces for decorative and practical use, including figures, umbrella stands, wall pockets, bowls, jugs and vases. The firm also produced some often highly amusing novelty objects, including realistically modelled biscuits and nuts (usually walnuts) on dishes, and ashtrays with simulated pipes or cigars resting on the rims. The most desirable objects in Bretby's repertoire are the figural subjects; Tooth is known to have modelled a set of gypsy children from life. Other popular items include jardinières grasped by seated apes, and small black cats. Bretby wares are always marked.

The vase shown *above*, with its dark brown glaze and floral decoration painted on slips, illustrates a desirable type of early Bretby ware. Apart from flowers in autumnal colours, characteristic motifs include foliage or insects, sometimes applied using a light-coloured clay. Other favourite monochrome glazes used in many early pieces included a rich, amber colour and *sang-de-boeuf*, (which has a reddish tone).
* Early pieces are marked with an impressed sunburst motif above the word, "Bretby". From 1891, the mark incorporated the word, "England"; 20thC pieces are marked "made in England". The firm ceased producing art pottery in 1920.

Later Bretby ware

The pair of vases shown in the main picture is an example of the high quality of anatomical drawing often displayed in later Bretby ware (c.1895-1900). The birds are coated with a semi-matt glaze which contrasts with the irregular, streaky glaze on the bamboo stalks. The pair is well-balanced but not identical, another characteristic of Bretby design. Japanese figures and animals and birds in high or low relief appeared on many later pieces; imitation bamboo was part of a range of realistic effects which also included bronze, hammered copper or steel. Art Nouveau designs also proved a strong influence on Bretby's pottery in the late 1890s.

BURMANTOFTS (English, 1858-1904)

Another leading English manufacturer of art pottery, the firm of Burmantofts was founded by Messrs. Wilcox & Co. and was based near Leeds in Yorkshire. At first it concentrated on architectural terracotta (such as drainpipes) and only produced art pottery from 1880.

Burmantofts art pottery was made of earthenware from clay mined from the factory site, covered with feldspathic glazes and fired to high temperatures to make the body extremely hard. The firm produced decorative tiles, vases, bowls and jardinières well as pedestals and some tableware. Among the most notable early pieces were a series of bottles and jars resembling Japanese or African gourd water vessels, nests of small jars fastened together, and "pilgrim" bottles which could be suspended by a cord.

Typical Burmantofts pottery was covered in monochrome or multiple streaked glazes in *sang-de-boeuf*, orange, yellow, lime-green or turquoise. Other examples of the firm's glazes include copper or silver lustre over dark red or blue ground colours. Some objects were hand-painted and these usually have smooth surfaces.
* Later Burmantofts wares were retailed under the name of the Leeds Fireclay Company.

The most desirable Burmantofts wares are probably those which, like the vase shown *above*, are decorated with an Iznik-type palette (see p.46-7). Typically, it uses intricate scrollwork and stylized flowers together with, in this case, cherubs and bearded men. Pieces are marked on the base with the pottery's name in full or the monogram BF.

MARTIN BROTHERS

*A Martin Brothers stoneware tobacco jar and cover
1893; ht 13in/32.5cm; value code C*

Identification checklist for Martin Brothers stoneware
1. Is the piece stoneware?
2. Is it salt-glazed?
3. Is it signed and dated on the underside?
4. Is it hand-thrown (rather than slip cast)?
5. Are dominant colours earthy, mainly brown, green and blue?
6. If a tobacco jar, is it grotesque or animal in form?
7. Is any surface decoration painted or sgraffito (incised)?
8. Does any painted decoration feature birds, grasses or foliage?
9. If a miniature, does it relate to a known larger version?

Martin Brothers (English, 1873-1914)
The Martin brothers (Robert Wallace, Charles Douglas, Walter Frazer and Edwin Bruce) set up their first art pottery studio in Fulham, London, ostensibly under the leadership of Robert, although their work was collaborative. At the Lambeth School of Art, Robert learned the method of salt-glazing stoneware

which became the Martin Brothers hallmark. The firm produced mainly hand-thrown jugs and vases with a distinctly Arts and Crafts feel, some of which are of grotesque form. The tobacco jar shown here is a grotesque and pensive bird, a favourite design. The firm also produced a series of face jugs, many with a jocular moonbeam grin, in buff or grey stoneware. Chess pieces were another favoured form. Some pieces represent human figures, perhaps a barrister. Despite their rarity, these are not as sought-after today as the birds.

Marks

All Martin wares are hand-incised on the underside with the name and address of the maker and the date of production. The most sought-after pieces, made before 1873, are marked "Fulham". Later pieces are marked "London & Southall". "Bros" or "Brothers" was added in 1882. No fakes or reproductions are known.

Painted decoration tends to be naturalistic, dominated by grasses, foliage, butterflies and birds. In late 19thC wares, the Japanese inspiration is apparent, as in the vase *above*, from c.1890.
* The gently concave base is typical of Martin Brothers vases, the bases of which are always hand-finished rather than mechanically turned.
* However similar they may appear, no two Martin designs are exactly alike.

Decoration tends to be either painted or *sgraffito*. This baluster vase is a good example of their *sgraffito* work, here used horizontally between the lobed, "pod"-like verticals. The Martins produced a range of similar organic pod forms; these tend to be less popular than other Martinware. The pale green and puce coloured glaze of this example is unusual – the Martins tended to favour a more autumnal palette, of subdued blues, greens, browns and greys. However, they occasionally used bright colours, such as cobalt blue. Some pod wares have a distinctive speckled olive glaze.

The waisted neck, rectangular rim and angular handle of this stoneware jug, are common features of Martinware. The brothers often made miniature versions of their larger pieces and there are many examples of tiny vases and jugs based on this design. The market for these miniatures tends to be quite separate from that for the larger wares.

ELTON WARE

A slipware jug with a fish-shaped spout c..1885; ht15 ½ in/40cm; value code E.

Identification checklist for Elton Ware art pottery
1. Is the form sculptural and inventive, with a strong organic influence?
2. Is the piece of hand-made slipware?
3. Is it marked?
4. Does the ornamentation include incise-work, heavy enamels, or a combination of the two?
5. Is the piece glazed in more than one colour and perhaps marbled or streaked?
6. Are any spouts or handles given decorative treatment, perhaps sculpted to resemble human heads, masks, plants or animal bodies?
7. Do the motifs include asymmetrical sprays of flowers, or flowering branches and leaves?
8. Are the shape and decoration reminiscent of Japanese porcelain?

Elton Ware (English, 1881-1920)
Sir Edmund Elton (1846-1920) was an English baronet who devoted the latter part of his life to making art pottery. With the help of an under gardener, George F. Masters, who later became his chief assistant, Elton set up his workshop and kiln on his estate at Clevedon, Somerset, in 1880. He began trading as the Sunflower Pottery but changed the name to Elton Ware shortly before December 1882.

Although he received a great deal of expert advice, Elton was entirely self-taught. But from 1883 his wares were thought good enough to be shown at major exhibitions around the world where they won many medals, including the Universal Exhibition at Brussels (1897), Paris (1900) and Milan (1906).

He concentrated on purely decorative art pottery, including vases, jugs and cups and covers. His forms were extremely inventive if not always exclusive, for Elton was more interested in creating new and challenging forms than in repeating designs he was sure of. In fact, he experimented so much that the quality of his output always fluctuated.

Although his wares were usually unique, he would sometimes create different versions of the same idea. One example is the fish-headed jug illustrated in the main picture, a type which Elton transformed some years later by coating it with one of the crackled lustre glazes for which he became famous after 1902.
* The gold and silver lustre wares are the most collectable of all Elton's products.
* All pieces are hand-made.

Note
The fish-headed jug was not exclusive to Elton, but was made by several other small West Country firms. If in doubt, collectors should look for a mark on the underside.

Early glazes were often swirled over the surface to achieve a marbled effect, as in the slipware vase, *above*.
* Two main sources of inspiration were Japanese metalwork and ancient Romano-British pottery: the looped handles of this vase can be traced to ancient pottery vessels which were made to be suspended as well as to stand upright.

Dating point
Pieces decorated with lustre or crackle glazes, or those with openwork necks are post-1902.

Marks
These are painted and sometimes impressed, and they vary from a monogram "E" for Elton, to "E. H. Elton" or "Elton Clevedon" with or without a datemark. George Masters sometimes marked pieces he had decorated himself with his initials, "G F M".
* From 1920, following the death of Edmund Elton, a painted "X" was added after the name.

This slim, gourd-shaped vase is an adaptation of a Japanese drinkng vessel. The glaze is a streaked flambe type favoured by the Chinese. The use of incised and heavily enamelled decoration is typical of Elton's pottery before 1902. However, the combination of dark onglaze enamels over an even darker underlying glaze has never been popular, and wares with this sort of colouring are among the least desirable.

Pieces with extravagant shapes and colourful decoration are the most collectable. The organic spout of the jug *above*, derived from the shape of a bird, is highly original and therefore desirable.
* White Oriental-type *prunus* flowers, often asymmetrically placed as here, were popular not only with Elton but with a number of other potters of the period.

DELLA ROBBIA

A Della Robbia vase
c.1898; ht 13in/34cm; value code F

Identification checklist for Della Robbia ceramics
1. Do any glazed motifs have incised outlines?
2. Does the decoration include interwoven plant forms, Pre-Raphaelite figures, amphibians or fish?
3. Are the thin glazes uneven?
4. Is the body of the piece cream-coloured with a pale blue-green glaze?
5. Is the piece marked?
6. Is it all-over decorated?
7. Does it have an uneven surface?

Della Robbia (English, 1894-1906)
The Della Robbia Pottery produced ceramics at Birkenhead between 1894 and 1906 (with an interval c.1901). The founders, including Harold Rathbone and Conrad Dressler, were designers who shared the ideals of "honest labour" and individualism

expounded by the Arts and Crafts
movement. The firm mass-
produced hand-thrown art
pottery, concentrating in the early
days on architectural (notably
church) ornamentation, inspired
by the work of the 15thC
Florentine artist, Luca Della
Robbia. Later products include
household objects such as jugs,
vases, clock cases and spoon
warmers, as well as decorative
figurines. Decoration is generally
sgraffito (incised) and forms are
strongly organic. Later wares, like
that shown *left*, tend to show a
strong Art Nouveau element.

This "Algerian" vase, *above*, has
one of the most common Della
Robbia shapes. The bulbous body
and curving handles are typical.
Other decorative styles favoured
by the firm were inspired by
Islamic, Celtic and heraldic
patterns and were applied to
Italianate and classical types of
jugs, vases and chargers.

Marks
The company mark, *above*, is
usually incised. Individual
decorators often added their own
mark, generally as painted or
incised initials. Around 80 designers'
marks have been identified.

Decorative techniques
Della Robbia pieces generally
display a pale blue-green glaze on
a cream earthenware body and,
being hand-thrown, have a rough
surface. Colours tend to be
harmonious, and the washes
uneven. The most characteristic
decorative technique employed
by the firm was a variation of
Italian majolica, with lead glazes,
instead of tin, applied over a white
slip. A *sgraffito* line was used to
outline glazed areas.
   Other decorative techniques
used include moulding, painting
and applied relief. Designs always
cover the entire surface of the
piece and palettes always include
at least two colours. The enamels
are distinctive and similar to those
employed by Doulton's faience
department at their Lambeth
studios (see pp.76-8).
   Della Robbia employed a large
number of artists, including many
women. The Algerian vase, *right*,
was decorated by Liz Wilkins and
bears her painted monogram.
All wares are desirable today
although they vary in quality.
Early pieces are often fragile
owing to the use of porous clay.

Motifs
Before 1895, no consistency of
motifs can be identified. From
1898, Carlo Manzoni, an Italian
sculptor, ran the architectural
department of Della Robbia, and
popularized strongly geometric
designs. From c.1898, these gave
way to interwoven organic plant
shapes. Other common subjects
include:
* fish
* amphibians
* animals
* figural subjects (see the tile
panels *below*).

Human figures and angels
inspired by Renaissance,
Medieval or Pre-Raphaelite
portraits were common: the tile
panels *above* show *The first day of
creation* and *The third day of
creation*. They are part of a series
of six based on a design by
Edward Burne-Jones.

WEMYSS

A Wemyss pig decorated with cabbage roses by Karel Nekola
c.1899-1914; ht 12 ¹/₂ in/32cm; value code C/D

Identification checklist for Wemyss ware
1. If the piece is a figurine, does it represent an animal such as a pig, a bulldog, a cat or a rabbit?
2. Is it pottery?
3. Is it marked?
4. Is it hand-painted?
5. If it has more than one colour, does the palette include greens, pinks, browns, or purples?
6. If it is a piece of table or bathroom ware, is there a red or blue border around the rim?

Wemyss (Scottish, 1817-1930)
Wemyss ware was named after Wemyss Castle in Fife, Scotland, and was made at the Fife Pottery from 1880.

For the first three years, the new product struggled to find an identity, but in 1883, the owner brought in Karel Nekola, a Bohemian artist who quickly applied his personal style to the wares, giving them simple, solid forms but highly distinctive decoration.

Thanks to Nekola, Wemyss pottery soon acquired a reputation for great exclusivity. Commissions came via Thomas Goode & Co., who acted as sole agents for Wemyss pottery, which they retailed from their prestigious shop in Mayfair, London.

Note
Owing to the pottery's use of low-temperature firing, pre-1930s wares are extremely fragile and should be handled with care. This method of firing also results in porous clay.

Beware
In 1930, the Fife Pottery closed and the Wemyss rights and moulds were sold to the Bovey Pottery Co. in Bovey Tracey, Devon, whose products are presently less collectable. Although their wares look very similar to authentic Wemyss pottery, Bovey used a much harder material. Nekola's son, Joseph, was their chief designer, but after he died in 1952, the company ceased production of Wemyss lookalikes altogether.

Types of ware

The range covers both useful and ornamental wares, which vary in size from buttons to garden seats. The firm produced jugs moulded and painted to resemble sailors or Scottish personalities, as well as wall plaques, dressing table sets, mugs, preserve jars, and so on.

From 1897-11, Nekola made commemorative souvenirs starting with a range of tableware celebrating Queen Victoria's Diamond Jubilee and ending with pieces made for George V's coronation. These pieces are very collectable.

Perhaps the most charming of all are the moulded pigs, such as that in the main picture, together with cats and rabbits, all of which were made in many different sizes to be used as door stops or ornaments on nursery shelves. Nekola also made a range of large vases that copy the shapes and the floral and figural designs on Chinese, Japanese and Islamic ceramics, but these are rare.

Decoration

The decoration on Wemyss ware is mainly concentrated in the painted areas, and the backgrounds are often white. Motifs vary widely but the most typical include sprays of brightly-painted and realistic fruits and flowers, animals, birds and insects, and fishing fleets. The palette tends to be restricted to pinks, greens, blacks, browns and purples.

This two-handled cup was made to a design by Nekola between c.1899-1914. Examples such as this, with its decoration of cocks and hens, are especially desirable, as are those depicting ducks in a landscape of reeds.
* Handles and rims are sometimes patterned or twisted and often have single-colour borders, at first

red, and later, red or blue. Finer rim lines usually denote a later date of manufacture.
* The palette is reminiscent of French faience.
* Another form of mug or cup made by the firm has frog motifs moulded on the inside.

Marks

Authentic Wemyss ware bears a maker's mark or "Thomas Goode & Co". Some pieces show the initials "RH" for Fife's owner, Robert Heron, as well as "Wemyss". On those pieces executed by Karel Nekola, the 'y' of the word Wemyss is elongated. Karel's son Joseph marked his best pieces with "Nekola pinxt".

The loving cup or tyg shown *above* was designed by Nekola between 1883-1900, and, like the pig, is decorated with one of his most popular themes: large, pink cabbage roses appear on many pieces, and are probably the firm's best-known motif.
* All the wares were hand-painted by Nekola and his assistants.

Common 19thC Wemyss marks

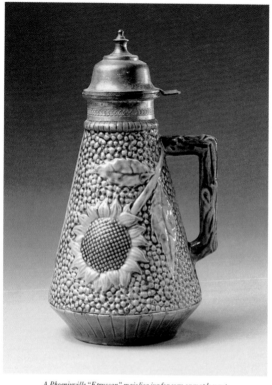

A Phoenixville "Etruscan" majolica jug for corn or maple syrup c.1880; ht 8 ¼ in/20cm; value code G

Identification checklist for Phoenixville majolica
1. Is the ware thickly potted?
2. Is the body crudely modelled?
3. Are the glazes more translucent than those typically used in English majolica (see pp.68-9).
4. Does the decoration include uniquely American motifs?
5. Does the colour scheme include blue, yellow, pink or green?
6. Does the object have an American function (for example, is it designed to hold an American product)?
7. Is the piece comparatively lightweight?

American majolica
The production of American majolica followed that of decorative ceramics in the United States as a whole, only really getting underway after the Centennial Exhibition in Philadelphia in 1876. The enormous commercial success of European and Japanese ornamental ceramics at this show provided the impetus for a massive expansion in the American ceramics industry which lasted until the First World War.

The Phoenixville Pottery (American, c.1867-1902)

The largest and most influential manufacturer of American majolica was Griffen, Smith and Hill's Phoenixville Pottery in Phoenixville, Pennsylvania. Established in c.1867, they produced the "Etruscan" majolica range from c.1879-91. By the mid-1880s, the pottery employed up to 400 people, and relied on local, grey clays.

The Etruscan range was mainly useful, glazed ware, heavily influenced by popular English designs which catered to a rapidly expanding domestic market. The pieces were generally far less ornamental than contemporary English majolica and included plates, dishes, humidors, pitchers, sardine boxes, tea wares and toilet sets. Many of them had identifiably American uses, such as the corn or maple syrup jug in the main picture. Its sunflower pattern was especially popular in Kansas, which is known as the "Sunflower State". Many of the Phoenixville designs show a strong Japanese influence as well.

All the pieces were inexpensive, and small examples were often given away as free gifts by American food manufacturers and distributors.
* A few ornamental vases were also made and are collectable today owing to their comparative rarity.
* The typical Etruscan body is thickly potted, light in weight and fired to a buff colour.

This pair of butter pat dishes is an example of the fashionable Etruscan shell and seaweed design, reminiscent of early 19thC Wedgwood. It is covered in a typically mottled glaze over intricate, realistic moulding. The lustrous effect was achieved by a controlled reducing atmosphere in the kilns, and was very unusual in Etruscan, or any other American majolica. The dishes are extremely collectable today.
* Later Etruscan wares were sparsely decorated or even undecorated.

Marks

Etruscan wares are often marked, usually with an impressed monogram of the initials GSH (for Griffen, Smith and Hill), and sometimes within a round border enclosing the name, Etruscan Majolica. This may be accompanied by an impressed design number with the prefix E, which may be the only mark present.

The crude marbled glazing or sponging on the base of this Etruscan majolica plate was a common feature of the Phoenixville wares.

This begonia leaf dish was made by Griffen, Smith and Hill in c.1880 and is one of the designs for which the firm is best-known. The palette of glazes is based on recipes developed for Staffordshire majolica in the 1850s and 1860s, but as the dish shows, the colour combinations were distinctly American.
* This dish design was both popular and inexpensive, and was produced in several sizes.

Other majolica makers

Other American manufacturers include Morley & Co., who made inexpensive majolica near Pittsburgh, Ohio, in c.1880, the Chesapeake Pottery, and several companies in and around Trenton, New Jersey, where the two most notable producers of majolica were the Eureka Pottery and Messrs. Taylor and Speeler.

ROOKWOOD

A Rookwood earthenware Japanese-style vase
1885; ht 6 ¹/₄ in/16cm; value code D

Identification checklist for Rookwood pottery
1. Is the piece art pottery?
2. Is it earthenware?
3. If marked, does it carry an artist's signature as well as the factory mark, and a date and shape number?
4. Are the decorative motifs Japanese or uniquely American, including American flora, fauna, landscapes or American Indians?
5. Is the ornament painted in coloured slip under a high, clear glaze or a matt glaze?
6. Does the slip consist of one main colour possibly blending from a lighter to a darker tone?
7. Is the ware heavily potted and slip cast?
8. Is the piece a vase, ewer or bowl of Japanese form?

Rookwood (American, 1880-1941)
Following the Philadelphia Centennial Exhibition, a number of American firms started to produce art pottery inspired by Japanese and European originals.

Rookwood was the largest and best-known of these companies. It was founded in Cincinnati by Maria Longworth Nichols, whose main aim was to produce ceramics that reflected Japanese standards and tastes.

Decoration

By 1882, Rookwood employed several decorators. Nichols specialized in painting Japanese flora and fauna in coloured slips under bright, clear glazes. One of Rookwood's chief designers was Marie Louise McLaughlin, who developed a decorative technique based on highly-glazed French Barbotine ware. She called this style "Cincinnati faience". The vase in the main picture was decorated by Anna M. Valentien.

Most of the firm's early pieces consisted of heavily potted, slip cast or thrown vases in dark background colours. These were usually of Japanese form and were often painted with Japanese or local flowers using the Barbotine technique.

In 1883, Rookwood refined its slip painting process to allow for a more even glaze and greater colour contrasts. Pieces decorated by this method were called "standard glaze ware", and were among the pottery's most successful products. Few early Rookwood pieces with pale glazes have survived, and these are now especially valuable.

Rookwood also manufactured matt and smear-glazed pottery in large quantities from c.1896. The earliest of these wares show incised decoration in the buff-coloured body as well as enamel ornament.

Between 1897 and c.1903, the firm made a series of Standard glaze vases depicting portraits of American Indians. The vase shown *above* is inscribed "Jumping Thunder" and was decorated by Matthew A. Daly. Today, these pieces are highly sought-after, especially those painted by William P. McDonald and Matthew A. Daly.

Marks

Until 1910, virtually all Rookwood pottery has a factory mark as well as a date and shape number. Marks may include an artist's monogram and an impressed code which indicates the clay colour (used from 1883-1900). Early examples are often impressed with the name, Rookwood, above a date, but from 1886 most have the monogram RP (see *below, left*).

Rookwood added a small flame over the monogram for each year from 1887 to 1900. The mark shown *above centre* is for 1887; later years could be identified by counting the number of flames. From 1900, the production date was shown by its last two digits in Roman numerals impressed below the monogram, *above right*.
* Some Rookwood pieces are marked with the word "second" or "give-away" which indicates a fault. This should be reflected in the price.

This vase was decorated for Rookwood by E. T. Hurley and is coated with a sea green glaze, one of several versions of the Standard glaze developed by the Pottery. The other glazes included "Iris", a pale, muted grey, and "gold stone", which was mottled. Many of these grounds are basically monochrome but often blend from light to dark tones of the same colour.

SCULPTURE

Effie Gray Millais, *a marble bust of the artist Sir John Millais' daughter by Sir John Edgar Boehm, court sculptor to Queen Victoria*

Early Victorian sculpture continued to be strongly influenced by the Neo-classical tastes that had flourished during the reigns of William IV and George IV. The work of the foremost classical-style sculptors, such as John Gibson, Sir Matthew Digby Wyatt, and the art medallist, E. W. Wyon, continued to reflect the work of the artist Canova (still active in Rome) and the Englishman, John Flaxman.

In the early 19thC, sculpture was life-size and in marble, and hence was the preserve of the rich and aristocratic. However, with the advent of the Cheverton reduction machine invented by the sculptor Benjamin Cheverton, small-scale and identically proportioned copies of existing sculptures could be made quite easily. The process was exhibited at the Great Exhibition of 1851 and thereafter demand for reduced sculptures grew rapidly. Soon, they could be bought fairly readily from art galleries. Those examples that bear the foundry seal "Cheverton reduction" are particularly collectable today.

Queen Victoria had a taste for the sentimental – her fondness for the romantic paintings of Landseer resulted in several being transformed into three-dimensional sculptures rendered in marble, bronze, terracotta and Parian ware. Similarly, her patronage of the work of sculptor Sir Edgar Boehm (1834-1890) ensured the popularity of romantic and sentimental sculpture, especially child subjects.

During the 1870s, a group of sculptors emerged who were determined to break the shackles of the Neo-classical past and, although the traditional classical subjects still remained popular, these were rendered with greater anatomical precision and in more immediate, impressionistic stances. Sculptors also attempted to capture more daring, and hitherto unrecorded moments and postures ignored or disdained by the Establishment. The sculptures are almost invariably bronze (although a few plaster and marble versions were made of some pieces). Most have a dark patination and are mounted on plain plinths, usually of the waisted socle (circular) type. The chief exponents of this New Sculpture included Frederick, Lord Leighton (see pp. 104-5), Sir Alfred Gilbert (see pp. 106-7) and Bertram Mackenneal (see pp. 108-9). The passion for realism and adherence to classical proportions, techniques and materials also inspired American sculptors of the period, notably Hiram Powers.

The work of the French animaliers (see pp. 100-103) found an appreciative market in Britain, but were rarely produced there. Although faking and copying of sculpture was not widespread at any time during the Victorian period, the greatest victims of these practices were the French animaliers, particularly the work of P. J. Mêne.

Various methods of casting were used during the period, the most popular being *cire perdue* (or "lost wax", a method of solid casting), sand-casting and electrotype. The electrotype process, popular between 1850 and 1870, involved the electrolytic application of a copper surface to a clay body, making the piece appear solid. Examples in this medium have not survived well and are not generally sought after today. In the sand-cast method, the piece is cast in sections, then joined and patinated.

The *cire perdue* process leads to unique castings; hence these pieces command a premium. Also, they tend to have an artistic spontaneity about them that is absent from the more clinical precision of sand-cast pieces, and are generally heavier and more detailed. Most examples bear either an incise-cut or stamped foundry mark stating that the piece is *cire perdue*. Unmarked *cire perdue* sculptures can be identified by the absence of the telltale joints characteristic of sand-cast pieces, although these joints are often disguised by the patination. Another useful point of comparison between the two is the base: the bases of sand-cast sculptures were cast separately and screwed or bolted in, whereas the bases of *cire perdue* pieces were cast in one.

THE NEO-CLASSICISTS

The Tinted Venus, *a wax-tinted marble sculpture by John Gibson c.1862; ht 69in/175cm; value code A*

Identification checklist for the sculpture of the Neo-classicists
1. Is the piece marble or, more rarely, bronze?
2. Is the subject of Anglo-Saxon or Northern European origin?
3. Is it sentimentalized?
4. Is the facial detail characteristically Victorian?
5. Is the subject naked or partially clad, with any drapery used primarily for modesty?
6. Is the pose somewhat stilted?
7. Does the surface retain traces of wax and colour?

John Gibson (English, 1790-1866)
John Gibson attempted to imitate precisely the subjects and methods of the Greek sculptors. The sculpting of his celebrated *Tinted Venus, above,* involved the Ancient Greek practice of covering the piece with a flesh-coloured wax overlay in an attempt to add a realistic skin-tone. His subjects are almost always classical or sentimental. The lack of originality of subject is often reflected in the execution of the piece, which can tend to be stiff and lifeless, with a contrived posture and stance. Faces are generally bland and characterless in their expression.

The Neo-classicists

Until the advent of the statuette in the mid-19thC, the Neo-classicists dominated the sculpture scene, with large subjects (sometimes greater than life-size), often classical maidens, usually rendered in marble. Today, these are regarded as somewhat formal and stilted. They are comparatively expensive and beyond the range of most collectors.

Edward Hodges Baily (English, 1788-1867)

A prolific artist and sculptor, Baily was responsible for many prestigious public commissions. His idealized subjects are often perfect embodiments of physique, fitness and youth. The young and athletic subject of *The Tired Hunter, above,* is typical. The proportions of the piece and the muscularity of the piece are classical, but the facial detail and hairstyle and the contrived positioning of the drapery are obviously Victorian. The base is characteristically simple.
* At 73in (186cm) high, *The Tired Hunter* is larger than life. However, generally Baily's sculptures are smaller than those of his contemporaries and thus tend to be more affordable.
* The greyhound is a typically Victorian subject in sculpture and painting, having been popularized as a domestic animal during the early 19thC.

James Wyatt II (English, 1808-1893)

A member of the hugely talented Wyatt dynasty, James Wyatt II began his career executing his father's sculptural designs, especially those with an equestrian aspect. His work tends to be more sentimental than austerely classical.

Lila Asleep, above, a portrait of the artist's daughter, is typically sentimental: the realistic and detailed face mark the figure out from the relative blandness of many Neo-classical subjects.
* The cushion base had been a popular feature of pre-Victorian sculpture. A contemporary designer, John Bell, produced several studies of children at prayer on similar cushion bases, examples of which were produced in Parian porcelain and marble.
* *Lila Asleep* was exhibited at the Royal Academy in London in 1838 and spawned a plethora of sleeping children and babes in the wood, a fashion which continued throughout the Victorian period.

John Henry Foley (English, 1818-74)

Often referred to as the last of the Neo-classicists, Foley's work hints at the New Sculpture to come (see p. 97). There are still strongly Neo-classical elements – for example, the convenient drapery and the rather stilted pose of the Norseman, *below.* Yet the figure displays a sense of drama and meaningful gesture that saves it from being lifeless.

Although it was produced in marble, this version of *The Norseman* is innovative in its use of bronze, a material rarely used during the early 19thC but which became very popular as the century progressed.

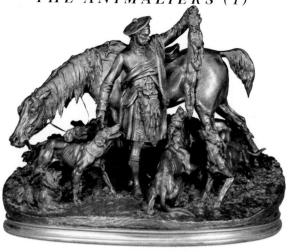

Le Prise du Renard-chasse en Ecosse (After the Hunt in Scotland), *by P. J. Mêne 1861; ht 21 1/4 in/54cm; value range varies, mainly B/C*

Identification checklist for the sculptures of the animaliers
1. Is the piece bronze (or, more rarely, iron)?
2. Is the facial detailing precise?
3. Is the casting of high definition?
4. Is the base, where elongated, of a uniform casting? (See facing page.)
5. Does it act as a naturalistic setting for the piece?
6. Is the piece signed?
7. Does it have a high-gloss patination?
8. Is the base perimeter plain and waisted?

Pierre Jule Mêne (French, 1810-79)
Perhaps the foremost 19thC animalier, and the most prolific, Mêne invariably demonstrates very precise detailing and an excellent sense of balance in his sculptures. These vary in size, although the figural groups rarely exceed two feet (61cm) in height. The smallest works can as little as 6 or 7in (15-17cm) high.
* Scottish subjects, such as that in the main picture were popular during the Victorian period, largely due to the enthusiasm of Prince Albert for the Scottish Highlands. Many other works of the period show idealized Scottish scenes or characters. Another version of this group exists in silver.

Mêne's best-known works are the groups. Many incorporate whippets, such as that shown *above*, with a greyhound, in the rich dark brown patination favoured by the animaliers generally and by Mêne in particular.
* Check that the piece is complete: in many cases the ball is missing.

Horses

Mêne's horse studies are very popular, especially those that incorporate a jockey, and all the more so if the subject is depicted high in the saddle, or "with jockey up". The horses invariably have a rectangular outline on the underside of the belly. This is because in the casting the piece is filled with fireclay which is subsequently emptied out, the hole then being covered with a plate. Occasionally, fragments of the fireclay get trapped inside, causing the piece to rattle when it is shaken.

* Animal sculptures tend to be extremely vulnerable, especially around any tails, ears or hooves. They should never be lifted by their legs as these are prone to snapping.

* Mêne's sculptures also exist as wax models, which were usually exhibited before the bronze casting was taken.

Mêne adapted a number of his figures to be used either singly or combined with others: the Scotsman, dog and fox in the main picture appear as a separate group, as illustrated *above*. Note that in this case the hat retains its feather.

* After his death a number of Mêne's sculptures were cast in bronze by A. N. Cain, Susse Frères and Ferdinand Barbedienne. These bear Mêne's signature and foundry mark, usually cast into the base. Some copies were made by Coalbrookdale and bear that name.

Antoine-Louis Barye (French, 1796-1875)

Barye was among the first of the animaliers and exhibited as early as the 1830s. Less prolific than Mêne, he used the *cire perdue* method to cast bronzes, resulting in unique casts (see p.97). His subjects tend to be spirited and shown in dramatic situations.

Marks

Apart from some early pieces which are unmarked, most of Barye's sculptures bear an incise-cast signature, usually in capital letters, obviously positioned. Most pieces are numbered. During the late 1840s and the 50s, some less successful castings were produced by Barye's creditor E. Martin. These are generally signed by Martin and not numbered. After Barye's death, some of his casts were edited by the Barbedienne foundry. These bear Barye's signature and the foundry mark but are not numbered.

Always powerful and well-cast, many of Barye's subjects are shown hunting other animals – for example, a hound chasing a stag, a tiger leaping on an antelope, or, as in the example *above*, a lion about to devour an owl.

As well as some stylized pieces of stately animals bearing noble subjects, Barye also sculpted naturalistically rendered, humbler creatures, such as that shown in *The Half-bred Horse, above*.

* He used several patinations on a piece to give a sense of movement and naturalism: in particular, different shades of brown were applied to a piece, or dark brown was combined with dark green.

THE ANIMALIERS (2)

Christophe Fratin (German-born, worked in France, 1800-64)

This sculptor is remembered for his highly individual treatment of animals, especially bears, in human situations and postures. The quality of casting and chiselling, and the attention to detail are excellent. His work was produced by a number of founders, including Susse Frères and E. Quesnel.

As well as bears, both anthropomorphic and naturalistic, Fratin also depicted other animals, such as monkeys and retrievers, some of which are thought to be parodies of notable people of the period. Some groups show violent scenes – for example, horses being attacked by wolves.

Fratin's early bronzes often had an irregular matt black patination; on these, some of the yellow metal beneath is evident through the patination and the recesses are very black. Later pieces often use a combination of patinations to achieve a lively effect. The reading bear shown *below* employs rich red and brown. Some pieces are gilded over the bronze. A notable example depicts a bear group of a dentist pulling a tooth from his patient.

Many of the sculptures are quite small – some as little as 5in (14cm) high.

Many of Fratin's animal sculptures are humorous, like this bronze bear, c.1850, reading a book and smoking a pipe. The "FRATIN" signature is visible on the front of the base.

Jules Moigniez (French, 1835-94)

Moigniez is most closely associated with his sculptures of birds, although he also produced several studies of dogs and other animals, some in a style similar to that of P. J. Mêne (see pp.100-1). However, his work is often more detailed than Mêne's, with less emphasis on the patination. Moigniez favoured brown patination, sometimes with gilt highlights. Bases are usually shallow and plinths waisted. Moigniez produced a series of caskets which incorporate birds and are also very collectable. All his work is signed.

This *Cockerel and Stoat, above,* is typical of Moigniez's distinctive treatment of his subjects and shows his accurate understanding of anatomy and plumage and his attention to detail – the feathers are ruffled and hair carefully delineated (rather than simply sketched in as a block). At 31 3/4in/80.5cm high, this is among Moigniez's larger works.
* Even fairly tame birds such as sparrows, convey an element of ferocity – for example, they are open-mouthed or poised to pounce. Such poses represent a departure from the gentle love birds favoured by earlier sculptors.
* Some Moigniez sculptures appear as embellishments to other items – for example, as finials on the covers of decorative vases.
* Moigniez also did a series of studies of dead game.

Emanuel Fremiet (French, 1824-1910)

Unlike Moigniez, Fremiet, although a keen observer of animals and birds, concentrated on these creatures' more endearing and sympathetic qualities, which perhaps explains why he was one of the most popular sculptors of his day. His work is harder to come by than that of the other sculptors shown on these two pages.

Friendly domestic groups form the bulk of Fremiet's output. This *Kitten and a Chick*, with dark brown patination and carefully

rendered detail – for example, the coat and feathers – is typical.
* As well as domestic animals, Fremiet depicted equestrian groups, and some wilder animals, such as gorillas. These pieces are generally later than the domestic sculptures: most date from the 1860s or later.
* Fremiet also designed a number of interiors.

The Bonheurs (brother and sister, French, Rosa: 1822-99; Isidore: 1827-1901)

During the 19thC Rosa was the better known of these two artists, although she produced fewer sculptures. As she was also a celebrated painter, her works were a favourite with Queen Victoria and Napoleon III. Her pieces are still more collectable, although often it is hard to distinguish between her work and Isidore's.

Rosa Bonheur designed a number of farm animals, including several bull studies such as the *Walking Bull* shown *above*, which admirably captures the strength and power of the animal. The dark brown patination and waisted base are typical of her sculptures.

Like Rosa, Isidore concentrated on strong or powerful studies of bulls, often in more dramatic postures than those of his sister. This prancing bull, *above*, is one of a pair with a standing bull, cast in three sizes. Isidore's subjects usually stand on a naturalistically rendered base, which bears his incise-cast signature and the stamp of the founder Hippolyte Peyrol. Patination is almost invariably brown.
* Successful as these bull studies are, Isidore Bonheur's most sought-after works today are his horse and jockey groups, some as high as 2ft (61cm). A number of fakes have been offered for sale. The bases on these are usually uneven and imprecise.

Animal sculpture fakes

In recent years there have been a massive number of fakes appearing on the market, most emanating from France and Canada, and many complete with fake signatures as well. These pieces can be identified in a number of ways:
* They lack the precision of detail of the originals.
* Many have a waxy type of patination which sems to attract and accumulate dirt, especially in

the crevices and incise-cast detail. On the originals the dust tends to be less apparent
* The bases lack signs of wear.
* The castings look modern, particularly from the underside, which is likely to appear unnaturally bright. Genuine old sculptures will have developed a light patination, even on the underside.
* The screws and bolts may be overbright if they are new or artificially rusted to suggest age.

LORD LEIGHTON

The Sluggard, *a bronze sculpture by Lord Leighton*
c.1890; ht 20 3/4 in/53cm; value code B

Identification checklist for the sculpture of Leighton
1. Is the subject figural, and in an unconventional pose?
2. Is the piece bronze, or less commonly copper?
3. Is the figure a nude?
4. Does the piece bear a signature and publisher's details?
5. Is it sand-cast?
6. Is the base a small, simple rectangle?
7. Is the patination dark, probably brown or green?

Frederick, Lord Leighton (English, 1830-96)

Leighton is regarded as the pioneer of the New Sculpture (see pp.96-7). Primarily a painter, he made clay models of his subjects to help in picture composition and was persuaded to cast his model, *Athlete Wrestling with a Python, below,* in bronze; a marble version followed which was then reduced in size and became the cast for his first commercially produced statuette.

Sculpted from a series of relaxed sittings by an artist's model, *The Sluggard,* (pictured *left*), shows a complete departure from the Neo-classical subjects of the earlier Victorians, having more in common with the Renaissance bronzes of the 16thC. It displays a true sense of movement, despite a lethargic facial expression. Versions exist in different sizes, with larger ones fetching a higher price. The rich chocolate brown patination is typical. Like most of Leighton's pieces, it bears the publisher's details: it is signed, entitled and inscribed "Published by Arthur Leslie Collie, 39B Old Bond Street, London May 1st 1890".

emphasis is on posture and the drama of the moment, rather than detail, and the effect is of a great sense of movement. The example pictured here is in bronze, but versions exist in copper.

A few of Leighton's subjects are given a humorous treatment. This portrait, showing a young girl taking fright from a toad, is an example. The posture is unusual and innovative, as is the facial expression which, although impressionistic, still displays more expression than earlier, Neo-classical works tend to.
* Like all Leighton's work, this piece was created using the sand-casting method (see p. 97), and displays the superbly light and thin casting that is typical of his work.
* The octagonal green marble base of this piece, representing as it does the bank of a stream, is unusual for Leighton: he tended to prefer simple, square and undecorated bases, like that of *The Sluggard.*

Athlete Wrestling with a Python, above, first exhibited at the Royal Academy in 1877, is cited by many authorities as being perhaps the earliest expression of the New Sculpture. The subjects – particularly the python – are simplified almost to the point of being impressionistic. The

Availability

As well as the statuettes shown here, Leighton also produced a number of larger sculptures, often in marble. Such pieces were comparatively expensive, and tended to be bought only by the wealthy. They are relatively scarce today, perhaps because many have been kept in the family of the original owner.

SIR ALFRED GILBERT

Perseus Arming, *a sculpture by Sir Alfred Gilbert*
c.1882; ht 14in/36cm; value code A/B

Identification checklist for the sculpture of Gilbert
1. Does the subject appear to display character and
physical presence?
2. Is the predominant material bronze, with a rich brown
patination?
3. Is the subject a mythological figure, probably Greek or
Roman, or more rarely, a contemporary figure?
4. If the sculpture is of classical inspiration, is the
subject's pose casual rather than formal?
5. If the subject is idealized rather than classical, are any
limbs slightly elongated but with realistic muscles?
6. Does the subject carry items symbolic of his or her
interest or occupation, or does the position of the arms
suggest that the piece was originally designed to carry
such an item, now lost?
7. If the subject is a likeness of a contemporary figure, is
the representation realistic, rather than idealized?
8. If the piece incorporates relief panels, are these in
copper, possibly highlighted with brilliant enamels?

Sir Alfred Gilbert (English, 1854-1934)

Regarded by many as the leading exponent of what the writer Edmund Gosse referred to at the time as the New Sculpture, Gilbert was one of the most public sculptors of the late Victorian era and remains so today by virtue of *Eros*, the Shaftesbury memorial in Piccadilly Circus in London. In an era when magnificent public ceremony and celebration were the order of the day, he received many public commissions, including several for the Royal Family. He worked mainly in bronze, although occasionally in aluminium. His sculptures are realistic, with fine muscular detail, and tend to be naturally, even casually, posed, unlike the more formal positioning of the earlier Neo-classicists.

Subjects include mythical and allegorical figures and saints, or well-known contemporary figures, some of which were said to convey the personality of the subject.

Having finished a monumental or commissioned piece, Gilbert tended to make several smaller, often miniature versions and it is these that are generally found at auction today. His later work, both monumental and miniature, tends to bring in other media – for example, enamel, or relief panels and plinths, occasionally executed using the process of copper electrotyping (see p. 97).
* Pieces often carry a foundry mark.

Cire-perdue ("lost wax") casting

The solid, seamless appearance of the piece in the main picture suggests that Gilbert used the *cire perdue*, or "lost wax", casting method (see pp. 96-7), which he preferred to the more modern and cheaper sand-casting method. Having made a piece, Gilbert tended to subtly alter subsequent re-casts or copies. This was sometimes done in order to accommodate a reduction in size or simply for variety — a sandal or a sword changes, the angle of the head is altered slightly. In the version of *Perseus Arming* in the main picture, the wings on the helmet are fully formed and face upwards and backwards, the right sandal is winged, and the sword blade is curved and shaped: however, examples exist with horizontal, forward-pointing helmet wings, unwinged sandals (or no sandals at all) and straight-bladed swords.

Icarus, above, was first exhibited at the Royal Academy in London in 1884 and is believed to be partly a self-portrait. This piece has the rich, chocolate brown patination characteristic of Gilbert's sculpture, and popular in the period generally.

Gilbert appears to have been preoccupied by adolescence, and the transition from adolescence to adulthood. His choice of Icarus and Perseus as subjects represents a mythological interpretation of this theme, as is *Tribute to Hymen, above*. Of all Gilbert's pieces, *Tribute to Hymen* was the most popular at the time and is the most likely to come up at auction today. The piece depicts a naked, pubescent girl holding variously a burner, a winged statue or a floral tribute to the God of Marriage, although these are often missing on examples found today.

107

BERTRAM MACKENNAL

Circe, *a bronze figure by Bertram Mackennal*
c.1893; ht 22 1/2 in/57cm; value code A

Identification checklist for the sculpture of Bertram
Mackennal
1. Is the subject a mythological figure, probably female,
with a robust, lithe and athletic form, and possibly
depicted with an element of symbolism?
2. Is the piece bronze (or, more rarely, marble)?
3. If a female, does the subject support a chignon hairstyle?
4. Is the anatomy of the human form realistically rendered?
5. Does the piece bear a foundry mark, perhaps
accompanied by Mackennal's signature and the date?
6. Is the base or plinth figured, possibly with naked male
and female forms entwined?
7. Is the patination dark brown?

**Sir Edgar Bertram Mackennal
(Australian, 1863-1931)**
Mackennal came to Europe in
1882. Studying and working
mainly in Paris, but also in London,
his style developed under the
influence of French Symbolism
and Romanticism. A popular
craftsman, he was commissioned
to design George V's coronation
medal, the obverse of the new

coinage and postage stamps. He is
best remembered for his
mythological sculptures, which
are particularly popular with
Australian collectors. He was also
commissioned to do some
maquettes for memorials, including
some mother and child groups and
bas-reliefs; these are less sought-
after. His work is not known to
have been copied or faked.

Note
* Most of Mackennal's sculptures are small statuettes although there is a life-size version of *Circe*.
* Pieces are usually in bronze; a few marble works have also been found.

Like Leighton (see pp.104-5), Mackennal sometimes featured classical subjects in unusual, even casual poses: here Diana is shown bandaging a wound. The piece is signed and dated, "B. Mackennal 1905" and bears the foundry mark "HOHWILLER FONDEUR".
* This sculpture is bronze but a version also exists in marble. The example here is 16$^{1}/_{2}$ in/42cm high but smaller examples are also known.

This bronze of *Salome* is typical of Mackennal's preference for dramatic sculptures with a strong female as the central figure. The treatment of the base, with its entwined snakes, was particularly innovative for its day (see *below*).

Bases and plinths
The bases and plinths of Mackennal's pieces are often unusual and inventive. Not content with the standard socle (plinth) base, he tended to decorate his with figures or motifs that reflected the theme of the piece. His original, life-size *Circe*, (of which the piece featured in the main picture is a smaller version), is mounted on a base depicting a *mêlée* of naked male and female figures. This caused a storm when the piece was exhibited at the Royal Academy in London in 1894 and eventually the base had to be covered in red baize so as not to "deprave or corrupt" the viewing public.

Makers and marks
Most pieces are signed and bear the mark of one of the two French foundries who published Mackennal's work – Grue et Jeune, whose stamp is circular. The other founder was Hohwiller (see *right*).
* Some pieces are titled – for example, *Salome*. The *Circe* sculpture is labelled "KIPKE", the Greek spelling of "Circe".

The patination of a piece should be in good order – that of the figure in the main picture is excellent, with a good sheen. However, this *Circe*, *above*, is badly weathered, probably from having been left outside or too near a fireplace, which has reduced its value. Bronze can be repatinated, but it is important that any such work be carried out professionally. If the quality of the work is good, a repatinated piece should hold its value. Recent repatination is fairly easy to detect, as it takes time to mellow to the deep warm colour of original patination.

SIR W. H. THORNYCROFT

Teucer, *a sculpture by Thornycroft*
c.1881; ht 30in/66cm; value code A

Identification checklist for the sculpture of Thornycroft
1. Does the piece depict a working man in a casual or resting position, or a classical subject with innovative detail (see *opposite*)?
2. Is the subject lean and athletic, with a sense of power?
3. Is the facial expression strongly defined?
4. Is the piece signed?
5. Is it bronze or plaster?
6. Is the patination dark, probably brown or green?

Note
Like other exponents of the New Sculpture (see pp.96-7), Thornycroft worked in plaster and bronze; his small pieces are almost invariably bronze, with a rich patination, usually brown or dark green. *Teucer, above* is a reduction of the life-size model exhibited at the Royal Academy, cast in plaster, in 1881 and in bronze in 1882 – Thornycroft tended to cast pieces in plaster first; hence replication was simple and a number of copies were made of each piece – 25 were cast of this edition, and a total of 288 of the lifesize plaster version.

Sir William Hamo Thornycroft (English, 1850-1925)

The son of a sculptor and paintress, Thornycroft originally attracted attention with a series of lifesize plaster statues of subjects drawn from Greek mythology. Smaller versions were later cast in bronze and issued in collectors' limited editions. His realistic approach to sculpture ensures his inclusion in that group of artisans called the New Sculptors (see p.96-7), who sought to break away from the stifling romanticism of the Neo-classical tradition and to establish a new, realistic identity within the medium. Although *Teucer, left* might be seen as a typically classical subject and pose, the quality of casting, the facial expression and the well-defined muscular tension redeem it from the blandness often associated with Neo-classical sculptures.

Exhibited in 1880 at the Royal Academy as a life-size plaster cast, *Artemis and her Hound, above,* was so well received as to have a lifesize marble version commissioned for the home of the Duke of Westminster. The novel arrangement of Artemis's gown and the revealing of her breast, lend this classical figure an originality symptomatic of the new movement in English sculpture.
* Thornycroft made some portrait bronzes to commission. These also appear in reduced size, most notably the memorial statue to General Gordon, killed at Khartoum in 1885.

Identification

Most models are well-known and reliably well-documented, and are often signed, dated, and even numbered. (*The Mower* is signed twice and dated twice – 1888 and 1890. The reason for this is not known.) Thornycroft's sculptures are not known to have been faked.

The Collie Foundry

Prior to the mid-19thC there had been no tradition of bronze foundry work in England, as there had been in Europe. The popularity of the bronze statuette led to the establishment of several foundries. Some of Thornycroft's pieces were published by Collie, a London-based foundry. Most of Collie's pieces are marked, some bearing the legend "Published by Arthur Leslie Collie".

The exhibition in 1884 of Thornycroft's life-sized plaster sculpture entitled *The Mower, above,* showed a break from the classical tradition, by depicting an ordinary working man. This would have been considered extremely unusual in its day. This version, with the scythe held pointing downwards, is not quite as free or innovative in style as some of the earlier versions, which tend to show the scythe resting on its handle rather than its blade.

JEWELRY

An amethyst cameo pendant with an enamel and diamond border

The Victorian period witnessed a revolt against the plainness that characterized jewelry of the George III period. An element of showiness was introduced that became increasingly pronounced as the century wore on. In Britain, many designs borrowed from the Continent of Europe, but were adapted to suit the British taste for heavier forms. Toward the end of the period styles became much lighter and more open, and often showed the influence of the Orient, sometimes becoming more angular.

The Continental influence was also important in the United States, especially during the second half of the 19thC. Forms were ornate and often heavily jewelled. As in Britain, jewellers also catered for the various revivalist movements.

The replacement of candlelight, first by gas lighting and then by electricity, had a big impact on styles: diamonds came into their own, taking advantage not only of the better lighting but also of improved cutting and mounting techniques. The coloured foil backings that had been used to deepen the colour of stones were no longer needed.

Cameos came back into fashion, in keeping with the

interest in all things renaissance. Both pendants and earrings were long, to complement the low necklines of the day. Fringed necklaces were also popular. Wrists were adorned with bracelets, or, especially from the 1880s, bangles. Jewelry was also worn in the hair – for example, as tiaras or even on strings of looped or plaited pearls. Earrings were *de rigueur* for the fashionable lady. Hang drops were very much in favour, the pendant type in the early part of the period gradually giving way to studs toward the end of the century.

Until c.1850 most jewelry was hand-made, but after that date machine techniques were frequently employed. Any hand-made items are particularly sought-after today.

Gold is measured in carats. The yellower the gold, the higher the carat and the greater the proportion of gold to metal – for example, 9 carat gold is one part gold to two parts metal. Most 19thC gold is 15 carat.

Some pieces are gilded, that is, are of base metal given a thin gold coating. Gilded pieces are difficult for the untrained eye to spot. However, they can sometimes be identified by the presence of a patch of a different colour where the gilding has worn off and exposed the metal beneath. To be certain, a jeweller or dealer may need to scrape the piece in an unobtrusive place and test the scraping with acid. Sadly, many good pieces have been ruined by being scraped in obvious places and these should be avoided.

Sets of jewelry were popular, and those that survive intact and in their original boxes command a premium. Note that any mark on the box or fitted case is more likely to be that of the retailer than the maker.

Many watches were worn on gold pendants, sometimes enamelled, engraved or embellished with diamonds. Diamond watches are collectable as jewelry, but others are sought-after only if they are by top makers. An exception is repeater watches, which strike the hour and the quarters, and very occasionally the minutes.

By the 19thC, men were wearing far less jewelry than ever before and the few items worn by them during this period were cravat pins, a few rings and watch chains.

Condition is an important factor. Avoid pieces that have been repaired with lead solder rather than gold solder, as lead looks ugly and untidy around the damaged area. On flexible (articulated) pieces examine the amount of wear at the links, especially at the joints of curved bracelets.

Collecting Victorian jewelry can be a minefield for the inexperienced buyer, especially as, with the exception of work by the top makers, very few pieces are marked. Collectors should always seek expert guidance, especially in the case of identifying stones as there are now many excellent copies and fakes on the market. Where marked, the mark is usually in a very obscure place – for example, on a hook or fitting, so it is also important to determine that such fittings are original to the piece. Provenance commands a premium and is usually a sign of quality.

MOURNING JEWELRY

A Victorian gold demi-parure (part-set) of hinged bangle, brooch and drop earrings c.1860; value code C

Identification checklist for mourning jewelry
1. Is black (or mauve) dominant in the colour scheme?
2. Is the black signified by onyx, jet or other black stones?
3. Is there a locket element or container for hair or a picture?
4. Does the piece incorporate pearls?
5. Does it bear engraved or enamelled initials?
6. Is it gold? (Rolled gold is also acceptable.)
7. If apparently a set, do all the components match in style of decoration and method of execution?
8. Do rings contain black or white enamel, or a combination of the two? (White is symbolic of the virginal state.)

Mourning jewelry

Mourning or memorial jewelry was as prolific during the Victorian era as it had been in the 17th and 18thC although in a more subtle form than the skulls and crossbones previously favoured. Unfashionable for a period, it is now very sought-after and can command high prices. It is characterized by its use of dark grounds and stones, especially jet, black or very dark blue enamel, and agate and onyx (which are the same stone, although the banded part is usually referred to as agate). Sometimes, a combination of these materials was used.
* Unlike enamel, onyx has a lustre.
* Black glass (or "French jet"), has a noticeably glassier texture than real jet.

Pearls

Pearls, symbolic of tears, were employed in many pieces of mourning jewelry. Like those in the main picture, they were cut in half and cemented or "pinch-set" into position, allowing for a closer fit to the mount. (The mount can be seen where the bottom pearl in the central star motif of the brooch is missing.)
* Although the missing pearl is only small, it can be costly to find a matching replacement.

Rings

Initialled mourning rings were sometimes commissioned by a dying person to be given to friends and family after their death. Thus, identical rings are not necessarily copies or reproductions.

Sets

Occasionally, mixed items are offered as sets. These can usually be detected on close examination of the materials and style of decoration used. The pieces in the main picture clearly belong together: they employ the same materials and style of decoration. However, the elements of the "set" shown above do not belong together: although both pieces have cabochon agates and a similar striped theme, only the brooch has a beaded border. Also, the enamelled angular mounts of the earrings are typical of a style that became popular c.1900, whereas the brooch has the typically rounded form of c.1880.

Flowers were used to good decorative effect against the dark enamelled background popular with this type of jewelry. Forget-me-nots, as in this mourning bangle, were very common.
* Examine hollow pieces carefully for any signs of damage as, being tubular (rather than flat), they are very difficult to repair.

This enamel brooch, c.1890, is also decorated with a forget-me-not but shows the lighter styles that were in vogue toward the end of the century, when mourning jewelry had begun to be phased out.
* The piece shows the damage to which enamel is susceptible. Low down, the brooch has been chipped and painted over. However, while it is possible to match the colour to a greater or lesser extent, the original surface cannot be invisibly repaired without stripping and re-enamelling the whole piece.

Hair jewelry

Memorial jewelry fashioned from hair came in several forms, including necklaces, earrings, as shown *above*, and bracelets. Sprays of hair also appear in lockets. In time, photographs replaced hair as a memory of the loved one. However, even into the 1870s shops still supplied do-it-yourself kits for customers to make up their own hair jewelry. Today, hair jewelry, which must be in good condition to have any value at all, is mostly bought for its academic interest.

PENDANTS AND BROOCHES

A foiled rock crystal and chrysolite openwork locket back brooch c.1840; lgth 2in/5cm; value code F.

Identification checklist for pendants and brooches
1. Is the piece dual-purpose, with a detachable loop?
2. Is it of 15 carat gold?
3. Is it fitted with a locket at the back, or does it have a locket element (i.e. a recess for hair or a picture)?
4. Is the piece in good condition, with no bruises?
5. If a pendant, does it consist of multiple elements?

Locket pendants and brooches
While not in the true sense mourning jewelry, most pendants and brooches of the Victorian era have small lockets in the back for holding a momento such as a lock of hair or a photograph. As the taste was for heavy jewelry, the inclusion of a locket was a good way to use the space created by raising the metal to give a chunky appearance. The symbolic padlock suspended from the example shown in the main picture would have contained the locket. The design of the piece was a type much favoured during the period. Cheaper examples were made for the masses in gilt metal with coloured glass replacing the semi-precious stones. Although less expensive than their gold counterparts, they are nevertheless collectable in

their own right.
* Most lockets are backed and have a piece of glass inside to protect the insert. However, closed lockets also have a hinged lid at the front, whereas open lockets have a glass front and no cover.
* Most pieces are dual purpose: a small hinged ring at the back of the brooch flicks up to form the loop for a chain. The brooch fitting, which is screwed into the centre of the back, can be removed when not in use.

Glass or semi-precious stones?
Although it can be very difficult for the untrained eye to determine whether a jewel is precious, semi-precious or glass, glass can often be identified by the presence of gas bubbles, which are visible under a magnifying glass.

Archeological discoveries were an important source of inspiration for brooch and pendant designs. The simulated wire and beadwork of the ancient Etruscans is shown to good effect in the bulla and locket with the cruciform motif *above*.
* Garnets were popular during the Victorian period, and although semi-precious, fetch high prices.

Many pieces of the period have hanging tassels, as in this oval locket pendant. It is crucial that all the tassels be intact, as they are easily damaged. Often, they were shut between the lid and the box while being stored.

Frosted and gilded finishes are closely associated with the Victorian period. The frosted matt appearance of this gold locket complements the diamond star motif. Frosted gilding is sometimes replaced by a polished surface: this will cause a drop in value.

Ear pendants were usually sold separately from other pieces of jewelry although some boxed sets exist. This part-set is in gold, but is more commonly found in silver as, being a popular design, it was copied in the less expensive metal to make it available to a wider market.
* Earrings were also made in stud form, but always for pierced ears. Many had pearls or garnets or were in the form of circles made up of turquoise. The pendant type is more popular today.
* English jewelry of the period is generally heavier in style than the Continental pieces that inspired them.

Condition
As with other types of jewelry, pendants and brooches are susceptible to wear, especially on the high spots. One way to repair damaged or worn areas is to flood the whole piece with gold, although the colour match would inevitably be imperfect.
* Wear on high spots may reveal the base metal beneath gilded pieces (see p. 113).

The spare fittings that enabled jewelry to be used for more than one purpose – for example, a brooch back, would have been kept beneath the silk cover of the box, so it is particularly important in this category of wares to have the original fittings and it is preferable to have the original box as well.

CAMEOS

An oval hardstone cameo, depicting a female head profile mounted as a brooch/pendant c.1880; lgth 2in/5cm; value code F.

Identification checklist for cameo jewelry
1. Is the cameo hardstone? (Shell is generally less valuable, see facing page).
2. Does it have a high gloss lustre?
3. Does it contain more than one colour?
4. Is the mount gold and relatively ornate?
5. If earrings, do the profiles face each other?
6. If dual-purpose, does the pendant loop match the rest of the mount?
7. Is the cameo hand-cut (see facing page)?

Cameos

Cameos became popular again in the 19thC with the revival of interest in the early Roman art of gem cutting. The best cameo-cutters were in Italy, and most worked in shell rather than hardstone, paring away the layers of the stone in order to form a picture, each layer revealing a different colour. Many Italian cameos were imported loose (unmounted) to England, where they were mounted. Some examples can still be found that were never mounted: a jeweller would make up the mount once the cameo had been chosen.

Dating
Although often hand-finished, most 20thC cameos and reproductions are machine-cut, giving them a mechanical appearance. 20thC cameos often

chalcedony, a form of quartz, and moulded glass. Chalcedony is sharper than moulded glass although the glass can be fine-cut making it difficult to distinguish between the two materials.

have clearly modern subjects. With the increasing interest in archeology, many cameos, especially the early ones, were inspired by early Roman examples of emperors and gods. This shell cameo of c.1840 shows the head of Jupiter above an eagle. Mounts followed the style of jewelry generally: this one dates from c.1880.
* Contemporary subjects, such as William IV, were also portrayed.

Shell or hardstone?
Hardstone cameos – those made from onyx or agate – are the most desirable, being harder than shell and more difficult to work with. With the best hardstone carving several differently coloured layers can be achieved, as in the piece in the main picture, where several layers of the agate have been pared away to form the flower for the hair. In order to tell whether a cameo is shell or hardstone, scratch the back of the piece – if it is shell the scratch mark will be apparent, if hardstone, the cameo will be unaffected. In addition, hardstone has a higher gloss than shell. As it is a soft material, prone to wear, shell is seldom used for cameo rings. Any shell cameos should be examined carefully for evidence of cracks, usually visible when the piece is held up to the light. High spots are also prone, and detail, such as strands of hair, may blur in time as the edges soften.

Other materials
A few cameos are made from more obscure materials, including moonstones. Some are made from

This chalcedony cameo is not very desirable: it is somewhat plain and of only one colour.
* Female subjects were, and still are, more popular than males. Designs were pre-set rather than specially commissioned.

Lava cameos
Cameos made from lava are probably the least popular variety, partly because they are usually in murky colours. However, the carvings are often delightful. The cutting is usually in very high relief, and thus prone to wear.

Good quality cameos are usually in a good surround. The best are in gold (or diamonds); gilt metal is also acceptable. Most are ornate and show signs of good quality workmanship: the hardstone cameo above, has an elaborate gold surround with pierced decoration.

Cameo earrings
Cameo pendant earrings are sought-after today. They were made in quantity and although many found today may be identical, they are not necessarily a pair: the profiles of a genuine pair will face each other.

DIAMOND JEWELRY

A set of diamond tiara stars
c.1870; lgth of largest 1¹/₂in/4cm; value code C

Identification checklist for diamond jewelry
1. Are the diamonds mounted in silver? (Gold is uncommon.)
2. If the surface metal is silver, has it a dark finish?
3. Are the diamonds cushion- or table-cut? (See p. 121.)
4. Do the motifs include stars, animals, snakes or insects?
5. Are open-set diamonds without a backing? (see *below.*)
6. If an earring, does it have wires for pierced ears?

Diamond jewelry
Jewelry with diamonds, occasionally combined with other stones, was popular in all forms in the 19thC. Value is determined as much by the overall decorative effect as by the quality of the diamonds. The quality of modern fakes is such that even experts have difficulty in distinguishing between a real diamond and a fake. However, paste stones, which were not necessarily intended to deceive, are gilded at the back (or backed with glass) to brighten the stones.

Diamonds were in closed (*above, bottom*) or open (*above, top*) settings. Closed settings, from the late 18th and early 19thC usually contain foil to add to the brilliance.

Diamond mounts
The type and method of mounting are a good aid to dating. All closed setting 19thC diamonds are mounted in either silver or gold, or, more often, with silver on gold. Platinum was not used until the 20thC.

If the mount is white metal and has a hard polished finish, it will either be platinum and thus 20thC, or will have been rhodium-plated, again, during the 20th, to give an old piece a modern appearance. However, such an alteration will detract from the value, as the distinctive feel of the individual stones will have been lost, and the piece will no longer be in its original state.

Silver is a softer metal than platinum and will not stand as much wear on the claws that hold the diamonds in place. However, its advantage is that the individual stones show up better against it, as it naturally darkens with age. Silver that has acquired this dark patina should not be cleaned, as the character of the piece would be destroyed temporarily, although in time it will darken again. Compare the silver and platinum mounts, *opposite.*

The diamonds of the brooch on the *left* have been set into silver which has darkened with age, making them stand out brightly from their setting. Those in the ring on the *right* have been reset into an obviously more modern 1920s platinum surround.

Diamond cuts

Diamond jewelry can also be dated by the cut of the diamonds. This is particularly important as some Victorian diamonds have been reset into platinum mounts.

The principal forms of cutting used in the Victorian period were rose-cutting, brilliant-cutting, and cushion or table-cutting.

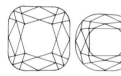

Cushion-shaped

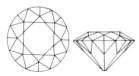

Old (Victorian) brilliant-cut

Modern brilliant cut

Rose-cut diamonds are chips from a larger diamond, flat at the back and faceted at the front. Modern diamonds are brilliant-cut but with more facets than Victorian "old" brilliant-cut diamonds. Old Victorian cuts have a visible spot in the centre.

Symbolism featured strongly in diamond jewelry. Necklaces in the form of a snake swallowing its own tail – a symbol of unity and eternity – abound. The snakes were decorated in a variety of stones, including diamonds. The example *above* has rose-diamond and blue enamel decoration.

Toward the end of the century, birds, butterflies and a range of other animals all became popular. Double-wing butterfly brooches were often made in a number of different stones: that shown *above* combines diamonds and sapphires.
* The butterfly is an ancient good luck symbol; wings were a popular Pre-Raphaelite motif.
* Stars, like those in the main picture, were popular in the period, and were often used to adorn a tiara or hair comb. Usually, these pieces could also be worn individually as brooches.
* Other popular Victorian subjects include:
* jockeys
* horseshoes.

Messages in stones

A popular Victorian practice was to spell out words using the initial letter of the colours chosen. The most common word is R.E.G.A.R.D. (made up of a ruby, emerald, garnet, amethyst, another ruby and a diamond). Alternatively, a piece might simply incorporate a bar with the initials in diamonds or other stones of the owner or recipient. These are obviously of more limited appeal.

121

A Tiffany enamelled brooch set with two natural pearls
c.1885; value code B/C

Identification checklist for Tiffany jewelry
1. Is the piece marked?
2. Is the item of a very high standard of design and execution?
3. Is the design in the contemporary taste for revivalism or realism?
4. If the item is composed of diamonds, is there a profusion of them?
5. Is the setting gold, perhaps incorporating floral motifs?
6. Is the gold 14 carat or higher?
7. Are silver mounts impressed with the word "sterling"?

Tiffany & Co. (American, 1837-present)

Although several American companies sold jewelry in the 19thC, none could compare with Tiffany in the quality and range of their products.

Founded by Charles Louis Tiffany (1812-1902) and John B. Mill Young, the firm started as Tiffany, Young & Ellis, a modest New York store that sold small, decorative objects imported from Europe and the Far East. Within a few years, the firm had gained a reputation for supplying its customers with high quality gemstones and commissioning ornate, modern jewelry from German and French goldsmiths.

By the early 1850s, the company, now known as Tiffany & Co., had moved to showrooms on Broadway, and during the last half of the century, it offered fashionable accessories, silverware (see pp.138-9) and many other kinds of desirable wares as well as jewelry.

In 1868, Tiffany opened branches in Paris, Geneva (where watches were made exclusively for the firm) and London.

The firm established its standards of excellence by commissioning designs in the form of working drawings from top American and foreign craftsmen as well as its own staff.

Designs

Tiffany's jewelry struck a balance between the demand for luxury, intrinsic value and modern design. But it also made its name by offering a range of multi-cultural styles which looked to the past as well as the present. The range included:

* Gothic, Rococo, Louis XVI and Renaissance designs, seen in watches as well as jewelry. The brooch illustrated in the main picture is based on a drawing by Holbein.
* Classical antiquity, including Greek, Roman, Pharaonic and Etruscan models.
* Persian and Moorish-influenced designs.
* European Art Nouveau-inspired designs. After the Paris Exposition Universelle of 1889, Tiffany quickly adopted this popular European style.
* American motifs. By the 1890s, the firm was orientated much more strongly towards indigenous American designs and materials than previously.
* realistically modelled flowers, insects and animals.

From about 1860, the firm thoroughly exploited the contemporary taste for verisimilitude. Such designs were usually made into brooches and clips on a gold frame which had been set with small diamonds or coloured gemstones and set against a polychrome, vitreous enamel. The diamonds were often in foliate settings on floral gold mounts. Many of the stones were obtained from the European aristocracy who sold their jewels under the threat of destitution, but they also came from newly discovered mines.

Stars were popular on both sides of the Atlantic in the 19thC. This diamond starburst brooch with its densely-packed stones is a typical Tiffany design, and was made in c.1885. The centre stone is of Tiffany's typically generous size, and the diamonds are set in silver mounts with a gold back.

Marks

Most jewelry and *objets vertu* made by Tiffany since 1868 are impressed with the firm's stamp and relevant metal marks.

Other leading makers

Tiffany's biggest rival was Shreve, Crump & Low, who manufactured jewelry and luxury items in Boston, Massachusetts, throughout the 19thC. Theodore B. Starr and Herman Marcus, based in New York City, and Bailey, Banks & Biddle of Philadelphia (established 1878) were all prominent jewelry makers and retailers in the 19thC, although none of them achieved Tiffany's status.

Starr and Marcus made especially fine enamel pieces including *plique à jour* brooches in Art Nouveau designs.

SILVER AND METALWORK

*A pair of Victorian silver-mounted frosted glass claret jugs by
Mortimer and Hunt, 1840-1*

During the early 19thC, silverwork remained heavily
influenced by the Georgian Neo-classical, although there was
a move towards naturalism during the later years of the reign
of William IV. By the 1840s, this had developed into the more
Rococo style that had its heyday at around the time of the
Great Exhibition in 1851, and which continued to find a
market well into the 20thC. The 1850s witnessed a great
revival in Renaissance silver, when pieces tended to display a
distinctly French influence, and were thus large-scale,
elaborate and expensive. After the Great Exhibition, this
disposition towards luxury items gave way to a new
preoccupation with less ornate pieces, coupled with an
interest in combining beauty with function.

The Victorian fondness for Japanese-style art is evident in
the motifs that decorate much silver and silver plate after
1870. This trend culminated in the simplification of design
and integration of form and function typified by the work of
Christopher Dresser (see pp. 130-1).

The influence of the Japanese style was particularly
important in the United States, especially after the
Philadelphia Centennial exhibition of 1876. Some American
factories produced very high quality silver, and, unlike other
areas of design, the American public considered their home-
produced silver to be equally desirable, if not preferable to,
European wares.

Towards the end of the century, the Crafts Guilds

produced hand-made silver using traditional techniques. Most of their work was executed in solid silver and, being hand-made, tended to be prohibitively expensive. To a great extent these pieces were passed over in favour of Liberty's less expensive ranges of Cymric silver and Tudric pewter, which were mass-produced but hand-finished.

Perhaps the most significant development in metalwares of this period was the fast and relatively inexpensive technique of electroplating, whereby silver was applied over a copper or nickel alloy. Thus silver plate, if not solid silver, was brought within the buying range of a far greater number of people. Wares are usually stamped EPNS for electro-plated nickel silver. Much contemporary electroplating was done using Britannia metal (an alloy of tin, antimony and copper) instead of nickel as the base, a process that became a staple of Sheffield manufacturers such as James Deakin and Son, James Yates, and Walker & Hall. Britannia metal is harder and more durable than pewter, which it resembles, and not as valuable. Examples are usually stamped EPBM (electro-plated Britannia metal).

The great iron foundries of the Midlands and the North responded with alacrity to the Victorian enthusiasm for the garden and produced wrought iron garden furniture in unprecedented quantities. Wrought iron was also brought indoors for the first time, in the form of bed frames, fireplace surrounds, boot scrapers and umbrella stands.

Brass and copper factories continued to produce staple domestic wares such as kettles, saucepans and other kitchen accessories, as well as church fittings. However, they also began to make larger items of furniture, such as beds, cots and light fittings.

Not all metalwork is marked, but many pieces carry the name of the maker. Contemporary documentation is sometimes available, especially for the work of leading firms.

In order to be legally called silver all British pieces must be hallmarked (although there are a few exceptions, see p. 133). The Victorian marks include a *lion passant* (which guarantees that a piece has met the standard of silver required), the date letter enclosed by a shield (which can be checked in a book of silver hallmarks), and, until 1890, the head of Queen Victoria, which indicated that duty had been paid on the item. Most pieces will also carry the maker's initials or marks. For American marks, see p. 139.

Masses of small and affordable items of Victorian silver can be found in antiques stores and auction houses today. The smaller pieces, which are within the means of most collectors and can be displayed effectively in most homes, are particularly popular.

Not all Victorian metalwork is collectable – for example, the plainer kitchenwares are unlikely ever to become valuable. However, ornate fire surrounds, attractive light fittings and unusual domestic wares are very collectable.

ELKINGTON & CO.

The "Milton Shield" designed for Elkington by Morel-Ladeuil 1867; lgth 33 ½ in/85cm; value code D

Identification checklist for Elkington silver and plate
1. Is the decoration based on classical, Renaissance or naturalistic designs?
2. Is the piece profusely decorated?
3. Is it marked?
4. Is it a piece of tableware, a decorative article for personal use, a display piece, or even a piece of furniture?
5. If plated, does it combine several plating techniques?
6. If several techniques are involved, are small nuts visible on the reverse where the separate components were joined?

Elkington & Co. (English, c.1829-1963 – merged)
The British electroplating industry was dominated by G. R. and Henry Elkington, who took out a patent for the process in 1840. Their success lay in their business acumen: by buying out their competitors and employing scientists as well as top designers, they were able to offer high quality goods at lower prices than the other leading makers. In 1842, the firm took on a third partner

and changed its name to Elkington, Mason & Co. Between 1840 and 1860, traditional, fused silver-plate was still often used for the main body of larger wares, but by the early 1860s, electroplate was respectable enough to be used on its own.

An even more refined technique called electrotyping was employed to make exact copies of original objects, and in the 1840s the firm produced do-it-yourself kits for the general public.

Types of ware

Elkington's earliest wares include small items such as snuff boxes, but during the 1840s, their range expanded to include tablewares, including candelabra, fruit dishes, chargers, tea urns and coffee pots, most of them highly ostentatious.
* Elkington used nickel as the base metal for ordinary pieces, but preferred copper for special wares.
* Electroplated items are often marked "EPNS" for electroplated nickel silver. An electroplated item is worth three to four times less than the same piece in silver.

The pitcher *above* is an example of Elkington's earlier decorative pieces which were largely inspired by French designs. It was made with a combination of plating and gilding.

Elkington designers

Many of the firm's early pieces were designed by a London silversmith, Benjamin Smith, who specialized in strikingly naturalistic motifs.

Another of Elkington's notable assistants was the Danish architect, Benjamin Schlick, who took moulds from classical and Renaissance antiquities to make tablewares and furniture which Elkington then reproduced in electroplate.

In 1859, the firm brought in two Continental artist-craftsmen, Leonard Morel-Ladeuil and A. A. Willms, both of whom were also inspired by Renaissance art. Their painstaking designs were mass-produced through a combination of electrotyping techniques which included gilding and damascening.
* Morel-Ladeuil's work was especially fine, and included display pieces such as the "Milton Shield" illustrated in the main picture.

Marks

Elkington used a complicated marking system. The earliest wares were marked "E & Co" crowned in a shield and the word "ELEC TRO PLATE" in three sections.

In 1841 and 1842 the mark was changed and a date number added. The series ran from 1-8.

From 1843, "E M & Co" was added in three separate shields.

From 1849, the date was shown by letters, beginning with K, and the alphabet started again in 1865, 1886 and 1912. Not all the letters were used. Wares made between 1842 and 1883, carry a diamond mark (see p. 184) which shows the date when the design was registered.

This oval mark (from the back of the "Milton Shield") certifies that the object was an approved copy of an original belonging to the Department of Science and Art (now the Victoria & Albert Museum in London). In 1853, the director, Henry Cole, allowed Elkington to reproduce antiquities and contemporary wares in the national collections, many of them exhibition pieces. Some of these items, such as the shield, were copied by Elkington on a huge scale. The firm also reproduced some pieces unofficially; these carry just the Elkington mark.

127

LEADING BRITISH SILVERSMITHS

A silver-gilt ewer by John S. Hunt
1853; ht 17in/41cm; value code C

Identification checklist for the work of the leading British silversmiths
1. Is the piece of obviously fine quality?
2. Does it show a French or Italian influence?
3. Is it hallmarked?
4. Does it incorporate naturalistic or realistic motifs?
5. Is the design inspired by the Renaissance?
6. Has the piece an elaborate form?
7. Is there a profusion of surface decoration?

Leading British silversmiths
During the Victorian period, silver tablewares were very fashionable and, for those who could afford it, there was no shortage of elaborate and often spectacular designs.

Ironically, the leading British silversmiths often employed French designers, but by the mid-1870s the combination of a general trade slump and strict hallmarking laws forced all these companies to make economies.

Although the Arts and Crafts Movement had a strong impact on British silverwares, classical, Renaissance and naturalistic styles prevailed throughout the 19thC.

The choice of available pieces included a wide range of tablewares including cow-creamers, salt cellars, tea urns, fish servers, punch and sweetmeat bowls, and magnificent centrepieces often incorporating candelabra or flower holders.
* Silver-gilt wares, like the ewer, are even more desirable than pure silver.
* Pieces retained in their original cases command a premium.

Rundell, Bridge & Rundell (English, founded 1804)

This London firm boasted the title of Royal Goldsmiths from 1804-43, although their wares were mainly silver or silver-gilt. Rundell's used the services of various designers including the English artist, John Flaxman, and outworkers such as Paul Storr, and Edward Barnard & Sons – one of the most important silver makers of the Victorian period.

Storr & Mortimer (English, 1822-c.1842)

Paul Storr was the most celebrated silversmith working in England during the 19thC, but his best-known pieces were large, Neo-classical silver-gilt wares produced for the Prince Regent before Victoria acceded to the throne. In partnership with John Mortimer until he retired in 1839, Storr signed his creations with his initials.

R. & S. Garrard (English, 1819-present)

Garrard's inherited Rundell's royal patronage in 1843, but preferred to be known as the Crown Jewellers, a title they hold to this day. The firm's 19thC wares are marked "RG". Like the work of the other leading silversmiths, although functional, pieces are also highly decorative.

This silver-gilt sweetmeat bowl and cover were made by Garrard in 1839. They are among the first examples of naturalism in silver, and although the composition is slightly unbalanced, the exuberance and inventiveness of the design makes them highly desirable nevertheless.

Hunt & Roskill (English, 1843-c.1939)

A successor to the firm of Storr & Mortimer, this company was headed by Storr's nephew, the silversmith, John Samuel Hunt. He recruited a French artist-craftsman, Antoine Vechte (1799-1868), whose forté was intricate embossing (or repoussé work) in imitation of elaborate Renaissance designs. His best pieces incorporated highly-detailed relief and three-dimensional figural compositions in oxidized silver to ornament large, presentation wares.

Hunt also borrowed heavily from ancient Italian motifs when he designed the ewer in the main picture.

This christening set – a very popular 19thC item – shows how Victorian decoration could smother form: the ornament just stops short of covering the functional areas. Hunt & Roskill made many fine, decorative wares and exhibition pieces such as this.

Charles and George Fox (English, 1849-1921)

This pair of wandering minstrel salt cellars was made in 1872 by C. T. & G. Fox, a London family firm who specialized in individual, high quality silverwares which were functional as well as decorative; many have novelty forms.

CHRISTOPHER DRESSER

A four-piece electroplated metal tea-set designed by Christopher Dresser for James Dixon 1880; ht of kettle 9in/23cm; value code B

Identification checklist for the silver and metalwork of Christopher Dresser
1. Is the form simple?
2. Is the piece devoid of surface decoration?
3. Is there a sense of balance and of form relating very closely to function?
4. Is the piece marked?
5. Do any legs consist of simple rods (usually, three)?
6. If a jug, does it have a rod handle?
7. Is there evidence of Japanese influence, especially in handles?
8. Are the bolts, rivets and other elements used in the construction, visible?
9. If electroplate, is the surface original (see opposite)?

Dr Christopher Dresser (Scottish, 1834-1904)
Initially a botanist, Dresser became a silver and metalwork designer in the early 1860s, and produced designs for a variety of firms including Elkington & Co., Hukin & Heath, James Dixon, Perry, Son & Co, Middleton & Heath and Benham & Froud (see pp.136-8). His knowledge of plants informs many of his designs. A visit to Japan also provided inspiration.

Many of his best silver and metalwork designs were produced during the 1880s but often, the preliminary drawings were made during the 1860s. His designs, which were considered revolutionary in their day, are devoid of surface decoration and instead concentrate on the marriage of form with function – for example, the handle and spout of teapots are at a perfect angle to meet the centre of gravity and thus pour with the minimum amount of effort.
He concentrated on tea services and small domestic useful wares.
* See also pp.49 and 81.

The use of ivory on this Hukin & Heath electroplated metal tureen is typical of Dresser: ivory, bone or ebonized wood were frequently employed for handles and finials to provide simple decorative appeal and to act as insulators. The rod form of handle, either vertical or horizontal, was one very much favoured by Dresser, especially on jugs, and reveals a Japanese influence.
* Supports are often simple struts or spikes, usually three.

Dresser's toast and letter racks are highly inventive. Many are of the simple bar and bead construction of this electroplated metal letter-rack, which is articulated – the central support is fixed but the three supports on either side are movable.

Marks
Dresser's pieces are invariably marked, usually stamped with the name or monogram of the manufacturer and often bearing a registration mark and style or registration number. Dresser is mostly, but not always, acknowledged as the designer. However, his designs are well-documented.

Note
Many Sheffield- and Birmingham-based manufacturers produced designs in the manner of Dresser. They may have been made by several of the craftsmen who executed Dresser's designs; they often bear the retailer's initials in the place of the manufacturer's.

Condition
Electroplate is very prone to wear. Usually, worn pieces suffer a loss in value but Dresser's pieces maintain their price whatever their condition because of the desirability of the forms. Restoration is possible but not advisable. Replating has a bright, whitish appearance. Old electroplate will have a mellow surface, with the scratches and signs of wear expected of a 19thC piece.

Collecting
* Although full services command a premium, single items are also very collectable. Silver usually commands a higher price than the same piece in electroplate.
* Pieces with curled scroll feet have never been as popular with collectors as those with rigid tripod strut feet.
* Many shapes exist in photograph form but the articles have never appeared on the market. However, the first examples of any hitherto unseen forms will be particularly eagerly sought after and can be expected to fetch top prices.
* Christopher Dresser designs are very popular in the United States.

An electroplated two-handled bowl with hinged cover, designed by Dresser.

Left: A Dresser decanter, produced in electroplate and in silver, glass and ivory; right: a "crow's foot" decanter, made in glass and electroplate or just electroplate.

C.R. ASHBEE AND THE GUILD OF HANDICRAFT

A silver cup and cover designed by C. R. Ashbee 1900; ht 8½ in/21cm; value code C

Identification checklist for the designs of Ashbee
1. Is the piece entirely hand-made?
2. Is it functional as well as decorative?
3. Does it incorporate open wirework, particularly in any handles?
4. Is any beaten decoration repoussé?
5. Does the piece incorporate semi-precious stones, such as turquoise or chrysoprase?
6. Is any decoration enamel?
7. Does the piece incorporate any glass lining, either plain or tinted?

The Guild of Handicraft (English, 1888-1908)
Established by C. R. Ashbee, the Guild of Handicraft consisted of artist-craftsmen who sought to perpetuate the pursuit of beauty in hand-crafting, in accordance with the ideals of medieval craft guilds. They worked mainly in wood and metal, to produce wares

that were functional as well as decorative; these included silverware, jewelry, furniture, leatherwork, and later, books. The Guild aimed to design and produce wares for the people, but in practice their pieces were exclusive, being hand-crafted.

Silverwares
With the exception of Ashbee, none of the Guildsmen had any experience of silversmithing, and Ashbee had no formal training. This is hard to believe when considering the competence displayed eventually by the Guildsmen. Early Guild silverware is regarded as pioneering; therefore, the earlier a piece the more desirable it is. Shapes are simple and have a hand-made appearance, with finely beaten surfaces. This is clearly visible on the base of the cup and cover in the main picture. Clear or tinted glass linings are often incorporated. The green lining of the cup and cover, was provided by the London glassworks of James Powell and Sons (see pp. 48-9), who supplied most of the glass used in Guild silverware.
* The Guild also produced electroplated pieces. Being hand-made, these are today as desirable as solid silver pieces and sometimes command the same price.

Charles Robert Ashbee (English, 1863-1942)
A leading figure in the Arts and Crafts movement, Ashbee was initially more an architect and designer than a craftsman, but appointed himself chief designer when he set up the Guild of Handicrafts in 1888. He designed silver, jewelry and some furniture.
* The other main Guild designer was Lewis Foreman Day.

The wirework on the handle of this dish, *above*, was used by many workshops, but none to such an extent as the Guild silversmiths. Close inspection of it reveals the finely beaten surface characteristic of hand-worked silver.

The decoration on the bowl is repoussé – that is, beaten in relief from the reverse side – and depicts the stylized foliage often found on Guild pieces.

Pieces often incorporate semi-precious stones. The buckle, *above*, designed by Ashbee for his wife, Janet, is set with four turquoises. Other stones used include chrysoprase (as in the handle of the silver dish), abalone, moonstone and pearl clusters. Enamelling is a common alternative to stones.

Roped or beaded rims, like that of the silver dish, *above*, are common Ashbee features. This example also has a characteristic wirework loop handle, here set with a chrysoprase, and displays the shallowness typical of much of the Guild's silverware. Many of Ashbee's designs were repeated; however, being hand-made, no two versions are identical.

Marks
Early pieces are unmarked. The initials "C.R.A" were used occasionally from 1896, when Ashbee registered his mark. Most pieces made after 1898 are marked "G of H Ld", but some of the guildsmen may have refused to submit their work for assay for fear of damaging their creations.

133

COALBROOKDALE

A Coalbrookdale cast-iron hallstand designed by Christopher Dresser 1867; ht 86in/219cm; wdth 53in/136cm; value code B/C

Identification checklist for Coalbrookdale metalwork
1. Is the piece cast-iron?
2. Is it ornately decorated?
3. Is the design symmetrical?
4. Is the decoration pierced into the casting?
5. Is the piece signed Coalbrookdale?
6. Is it well-cast with crisply rendered decoration?
7. Does the design reveal a sectional construction?

Note
Dresser designed a number of hallstands for Coalbrookdale in the same general style as that shown *above*, but with variations on the back supports; this one is unusual in having a mirror.

Coalbrookdale (English, 1709-present)

This leading British manufacturer of cast-iron wares, based in Shropshire, enjoyed a revival in the 1830s, when Abraham and Alfred Darby took over the running of the firm, which had fallen into decline under the management of their father Edmund.

The firm was innovative in that it used iron to produce beds (which had previously been made in wood). At first the iron beds were sometimes camouflaged to look like brass by being covered in brass foil and then varnished. Later in the century solid brass bedsteads became popular.

The successful use of iron for beds led to a greater awareness of the potential for using the medium in other ways and soon a variety of iron objects were available – for example, iron furniture for indoor and outdoor use, particularly sought-after following the new popularity of the conservatory. This type of furniture was often fanciful, ornately cast and sometimes decorated in relief with trailing ivy leaves. Seating often took the form of wooden splats (or, alternatively, thin iron straps). Another staple product for the firm was pub, or inn tables, which are usually round with central pedestal supports. Coalbrookdale also produced a series of small useful wares, including circular dishes, cast and pierced with Renaissance-type grotesques and arabesques. Most pieces were made in moulds on a commercial basis. Many items were exported to the United States and Europe.

Coalbrookdale's tour de force at the 1851 Exhibition were gates to large country house. After the exhibition these were rehoused (and remain) close to the present Albert Memorial in London.

Condition

Most cast-iron pieces found today are likely to have been repainted several times. Multiple layers of paint can dull definition. Occasionally, some of the original paint, which was probably black or white, may show through. Any rust will also be visible through the paint and is usually impossible to disguise completely. Pieces that appear to be in their original state command a premium, although these can be very difficult to identify.

Value point

Garden furniture has increased dramatically in value in the last five years. There are now special sales devoted to garden furniture and statuary.

Coalbrookdale designs by Dresser are the most collectable. However, the work of the firm's other notable designer, Alfred Stevens, is also sought-after. This cast-iron fire surround, 1857-60, is typical of Stevens's work in its pronounced sculptural quality. His work is less decorative and plainer than that of Dresser.
* Cast-iron fire surrounds proved popular in the Victorian period. At first the cast-iron was restricted to the surround, but later in the century it became an integral part of the fireplace.

Marks

Many wares bear the name Coalbrookdale on a pad applied to the underside of the piece at the centre. The patent mark (see p. 184) was also used after 1839. Some very similar decorative and sculptural ironwork was made in Russia. Although the marks are in Russian, they are very similar to those used by Coalbrookdale.

Left: *umbrella stand;* right: *detail from a fire surround, both pieces designed by Christopher Dresser*

*A Benson brass wall light with vaseline shade
c.1890; lgth 14in/35.5cm; value code E.*

Identification checklist for Benson wares
1. Is the design of futuristic or novel construction?
2. Is the item relatively free of decoration?
3. Is it stamped "Benson"?
4. Is it a light fitting, or tableware?
5. If a light fitting, is it made of several components
screwed together through a central axis?
6. Are any integral glass shades vaseline-tinted in the
manner of James Powell (see pp.48-9)?
7. Is the metal silver-plated, nickel, copper and/or brass?

William Arthur Smith Benson
(English, 1854-1924)
William Arthur Smith Benson was
a champion of industrial design.
Inspired by William Morris, he
opened a metalwork shop in
Hammersmith in 1880 and two
years later, moved to Chiswick.
He is best known for his light
fittings and tableware, but he also
designed wallpaper and furniture
for Morris, and fireplaces and
other architectural fittings. In 1887,
Benson opened a shop in London's
Bond Street, and his light fixtures
were also on sale in Paris at the
Maison de l'Art Nouveau. He
became Managing Director of
Morris's firm in 1896 while his own
company was still in production.

Light fixtures
The wall light *above* is an excellent
example of Benson's preference
for shapes which were both
functional and elegant. The
vaseline glass shade was probably
made by James Powell (see pp.
48-9), who supplied most of
Benson's glassware. The design
also shows Benson's liking for thin
metal structures screwed together
through a central axis.
Characteristically spare, the
ornamentation serves a practical as
well as a decorative purpose.
* Benson's range of light fittings
includes candlesticks, chandeliers
and lanterns, as well as wall lights.
Most designs were intended for
mass-production.

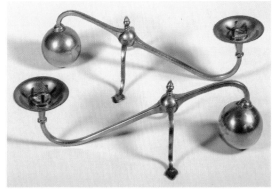

Tableware

Many of Benson's tea and coffee pots were made of brass combined with copper, although he also used plain and silver-plated nickel. Sometimes a decorative pattern was embossed onto the metal; knobs and handles were of wood and/or cane.

The most popular Benson candlesticks were those of Neo-gothic design and multiple construction. Balance was always an important consideration. Typically, the ball weights of the candlesticks *above* are not disguised, but have become integrated into the design.

BENHAM & FROUD (English, 1873-93)

Another English firm, Benham & Froud concentrated on household utility and kitchen wares. Most of their products are of little artistic merit and are not collectable, with the exception of those few designed by Christopher Dresser (see also pp.130-1), immediately identifiable by their original forms.

PERRY, SON & Co (English, 1876-83)

Dresser also designed household metalwares for the firm of Perry, Son & Co, one of several lighting manufacturers operating in and around Birmingham and Wolverhampton in the second half of the 19thC.

Christopher Dresser designed this copper and brass kettle for Benham & Froud in 1885. It demonstrates Dresser's extraordinary ability to make a useful object beautiful without the addition of any unnecessary ornament.
* The kettle is is stamped with the firm's usual cruciform trademark.
* A certain degree of damage is inevitable on wares that are useful as well as decorative and is usually considered acceptable, especially in the case of rare pieces such as this.

This brass chamberstick is stamped with Dresser's name and the firm's entwined rope mark. The stick also bears a registration lozenge which dates it firmly to 1883 (see p. 184).
* Perry sometimes painted their wares in duck egg blue or red. If painted, the most desirable objects are those which show the original colour. Retouchings should be obvious.
* Fakes of Perry wares are virtually unknown.

LEADING AMERICAN SILVERSMITHS

A Gorham ice bowl with polar bears
1870; ht 6 ¹/₄ in/17cm; lgth 10 ¹/₄ in/27.5cm; value code A

Identification checklist for Gorham and Tiffany silver and mixed metal wares

1. Are the forms and ornament inspired by Japanese designs, contemporary revivalism, notable events in American history, realism or Rococo art?
2. If based on a Japanese design, is it a highly stylized interpretation?
3. Is the piece marked with the maker's name?
4. Is the word STERLING impressed on the metal?
5. If the object is of mixed metals, do the metals include gold, copper or alloys as well as silver?
6. Is the metal gauge relatively thick, especially when compared to Continental silver?
7. If the decoration includes three-dimensional flora or fauna, are these well-modelled?
8. If made of Sterling silver, does the piece look hand-crafted?
9. Is the object or its ornament of relatively large scale?
10. Is the ornament profusely applied?

GORHAM (American, 1813-present)

This Rhode Island firm was the largest manufacturer of American silver in the 19thC. It owed its success to a combination of innovative and mechanical methods as well as high design standards.

Gorham's product range consisted mainly of useful and decorative tablewares, many of which were on a fairly large scale.

Rococo styles predominated, particularly on the hollow wares, which are often heavily chased or repoussé.

The firm's more progressive styles often relied on American motifs, notably those connected with the nationalist movement following the Civil War. The ice bowl in the main picture was made to commemorate the Alaska purchase of 1867.

Gorham was one of several firms

to combine silver or silver-plate with one or more other metals, usually gold, copper or alloys. This mixed metal *tazza*, made by Gorham in 1881, demonstrates the contemporary taste for Japanese design (following the Centennial Exhibition in 1876), as well as for a high degree of realism in the modelling: some of the leaves even show "worm holes".

* In 1868 Gorham adopted the Sterling standard for silver (925 parts silver to a thousand). This replaced the coin silver standard which had been only 900 parts silver to a thousand. (For marks, see *below right*.)

TIFFANY (American, 1837-present)

Although Gorham was more prolific, Tiffany (see also pp. 122-3) was largely responsible for the popularity of American silver and plated wares on the domestic market. The company also used more advanced techniques and higher quality silver than Gorham. Early Tiffany silver is mainly conventional or Rococo-revival flatware or useful hollow ware, especially tea and coffee services. However, throughout the second half of the 19thC the firm covered a more adventurous, revivalist repertoire of Pharaonic, Louis XVI, French Second Empire, Etruscan and Renaissance styles. Islamic and Moorish designs were also copied, and typically American motifs such as American Indians were used as well. Surfaces were often chased, engraved or inlaid, and highly realistic three-dimensional depictions of flora and fauna were common.

The Victorian taste for naturalism was also widely represented in Tiffany silver, with all types of flora and fauna including aquatic motifs and shells being represented.

* Tiffany adopted the English Sterling standard in 1852.

Some of Tiffany and Co's finest and most highly collected products are the "mixed metal" wares, such as this cylindrical vase, which shows Tiffany's interest in Japanese metal-smithing techniques: each of the applied panels is an example of a Japanese alloy coloured by patination. Also featured are a silver and copper wisteria vine and a copper dragonfly with gold wings. The base has a die-rolled border.

* Most Tiffany mixed metal wares were produced between 1878 and 1888. The pieces were generally small, single items such as vases, plates or covered boxes inspired by Japanese originals or the Aesthetic style.

* As well as the mixed metal wares, other extremely active Tiffany collecting areas include flatware (especially serving pieces) and *objets vertu*, such as match safes, some of which are also in gold.

Tiffany and Gorham marks

Gorham's earliest wares are often marked with a pseudo-English hallmark of a lion, an anchor and a Gothic "G". After 1863, their electroplated nickel silver wares usually bear an impressed anchor and the letters "EP" or "EPNS" Hollow ware was marked with year letters starting with a capital "A" from 1868, and the sequence was followed with ciphers from 1885.

Almost all Tiffany's silverware bears impressed marks including the firm's name and, from c.1859, the word "STERLING" (or "English Sterling"). A capital "M" for the designer, Edward C. Moore, was used until c.1891.

139

SMALL SILVER

Throughout the Victorian era a vast array of small artefacts and novel objects peculiar to the period were produced in silver, silver plate and Britannia metal. These include:

* pin cushions (often modelled in the form of birds)
* menu holders
* childrens' rattles (often with coral or ivory ring teethers)
* caddy spoons
* card cases (for visiting cards)
* nutmeg graters
* cabinet pieces, including dolls house furniture and miniature tea services
* wine labels
* vesta boxes (match holders)
* watch Alberts (a peculiarly Victorian name for a watch chain)
* chatelaines (worn by the lady of the house, this was a large decorative belt on which were hung keys, a notebook and pencil and other small useful items)
* glove stretchers
* watch cases and chains
* sovereign cases
* grape scissors
* sewing cases
* manicure sets
* silver buttons
* letter openers.

Many of these pieces can still be bought relatively inexpensively, especially those that are plate rather than solid silver.

Victorian era, and the early Victorians took them to new heights of decoration. The most elaborate were the "castle-top" examples, so called because of the castle embossed in high relief on the hinged cover. Famous ecclesiastical buildings were common alternatives to a "castle". The two examples *above*, both by Nathaniel Mills, the most prominent Victorian maker of castle-tops, show York Minster (1841), *top*, and St Paul's Cathedral (1852), *bottom*.

* Vinaigrettes often come in pairs but they are also available singly. A pair would fetch more than double the price of a single piece.
* Snuff boxes are similar in style to vinaigrettes, although they tend to be larger, and are available in silver, copper or brass, often with a gilt lining.

Pin trays, for use on the Victorian dressing table, often had the same type of raised decoration as vinaigrettes but on a larger scale. This example shows Windsor Castle.

Vinaigrettes (small containers for aromatic vinegar, smelling salts or perfume, carried to ward off unpleasant odours) first became popular during the later years of the Georgian period, but the fashion continued well into the

Short-handled spoons for use in tea caddies, known as caddy spoons, were first seen in the late 18thC. They come in a huge variety of shapes, often novel, usually with stamped or hand-embossed designs. The spoon *above* is in the shape of a hand – a popular Victorian motif in a variety of media including Parian ware and glass. Many caddy spoon handles are in the form of a leaf, with a bowl.

variety of stones, such as hardstone (*third from left*), bone, mother-of-pearl (*second from left*) and tortoiseshell (*far right*). "Everlasting" pencils (*above, bottom*), so-called because the lead, which runs the length of the shank of the pencil, can be continually renewed, were manufactured in large numbers: a prominent maker was Sampson Mordan. Common decorative elements include enamel (*fourth from right*), tiger's eye, bone, ceramic, applied metals and stones – the pencil *fifth from left* features a bloodstone.

Novelty cruets were extremely popular with the Victorians. Many were made by Thomas Wilkinson & Co.; the charming example *above*, is one of their registered designs. Owls were also common.
* The set is missing its glass or plated lift-out pepper and mustard pots. Nevertheless, it is sought-after for its novelty and decorative value. It is still possible to find components to complete such items, although they would still suffer a loss of value if the parts do not actually belong together.

Ornamental purses, often in the form of a little clutch bag, were a popular Victorian accessory. This example, of ivory with applied decoration in silver, is typical, although many examples are in silver, with no ivory.
* Many small bibles and prayer books were also decorated with applied silverwork, and were popular as christening presents. Alternatively, silver christening mugs were also given. Many of these are embellished with engraving.

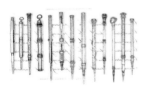

The creation of an international postal service towards the end of the 19thC led to the development of the fountain pen and to more widespread use of writing tools generally, particularly in the United States.
   Fountain pens were made in silver, silver-gilt and metal and are all collectable today. A selection are pictured *above, top*. Some, such as the twisted and inlaid gilt example pictured *centre*, were very elaborate. Common decorative elements include a

This Britannia metal inkwell is typical of the wares produced by James Deakin and Sons of Sheffield.
* Collectors should bear in mind that, once the metal begins to wear, it is very difficult to restore – replating has to be done at extremely low temperatures in order not to damage the piece.

TEXTILES

A pattern for Berlin woolwork published by Hertz and Wegener, Berlin, 1850/60.

The Victorian period saw great expansion in the textile industry. Innovative techniques such as power-loom weaving and machine-printing from engraved metal rollers accounted for the bulk of production, while traditional wood-block printing with alum and iron mordants and the vegetable dyes madder (red), indigo (blue) and quercitron (yellow) was mainly used for high quality floral chintzes and by William Morris (see pp. 154-5).

From 1810, a new range of mineral colours, including antimony orange (1817), manganese bronze (1823), and a solid green (instead of indigo "pencilled" over yellow) radically changed the look of printed textiles. Vivid coal-tar and aniline dyes, introduced in 1856, accentuated the change. The new, synthetic dyes often faded at different rates, altering the balance of the design.

The Victorians equated elaboration with beauty, and developed a bewildering variety of patterns. Their eclectic approach led to the revival of styles such as classical, Gothic, Renaissance, Elizabethan, Moorish or Alhambresque and Rococo. However, whilst borrowing heavily from the past, the leading designers created something essentially their own.

At the start of Victoria's reign, light colours predominated in glazed chintzes and silk damasks, but gradually colours became darker. Added to the use of heavier materials, such as velvets and brocatelles, this gave a richer, more sombre effect.

Patterns became more complex and exuberant with shaded architectural and *trompe l'oeil* motifs and ever more naturalistic flowers.

Fully pictorial, three-dimensional designs showing railway stations, the Crystal Palace, children and dogs, often surrounded by floral wreaths, reached their peak by the time of the 1851 Great Exhibition (see p.9). These motifs were criticized by design reformers. So, by the 1860s, simpler, flat patterns based on geometric or historic ornament began to predominate, with more restrained floral designs.

The Aesthetic period of the 1870s and 1880s (see pp.10-11) saw a strong Japanese influence, featuring flowers and birds, Japanese badges and other Oriental ornament. Tertiary, rather than primary colours, were preferred, including olive and greyish greens, yellows and pale turquoise. A number of Aesthetic designs, notably by A. H. Mackmurdo for the Century Guild in 1882-84, anticipated Art Nouveau, a style that was to predominate in the last decade of the 19thC. Textiles by Morris and his assistant, J.H. Dearle, spanned the period from the 1870s to the 1890s and were influential in Europe and the United States as well as at home. Liberty's textiles (see pp. 156-7) also had an astonishing success.

Until the 1870s, the most popular type of domestic embroidery was Berlin woolwork. First attempts to revive fine stitchery came from the Church, whose vestments and altar furnishings were designed by architects. From 1872, the Royal School of Needlework commissioned designs from Morris, Burne-Jones, Walter Crane, Selwyn Image and others, and within a few years "art needlework" had replaced Berlin woolwork. As with printed and woven textiles, English country flowers predominated, together with a revival of late 17th and early 18thC crewelwork with designs imitating the "tree of life" (wrongly called "Jacobean"), Japanese-style flora and fauna, the Italian Renaissance, and Cretan and Turkish embroideries. In the last decade of the 19thC, appliqué embroidery tended to replace fine stitchery. Samplers were often worked in coloured wools rather than in silk and were consequently coarser.

Both bobbin and needlepoint lace, together with crochet and braid laces, were made during the Victorian period. Designs for bobbin lace were drawn on vellum and placed on a pillow. Pins were placed upright along the lines of the pattern and the lace was built up by bobbin-weighted threads which were twisted around them. Needlepoint lace was made with needle and thread using buttonhole and other embroidery stitches, drawn thread work and cutwork. Competition from machine-made lace meant that hand-made lace tended to be made by amateurs rather than professionals. Simple, sprigged muslin Regency draperies were replaced by machine-made curtains with floral and pictorial designs. Machine embroidery in white thread was used on muslin and fine cotton for handkerchiefs, collars and cuffs, panels of christening robes and as the basis for machine-made lace.

EARLY AND HIGH VICTORIAN TEXTILES

A chalice veil of cream and gold silk damask by A. W. N. Pugin c.1848-50; 22½ x 22½ in/57 x 57cm; value code E.

Identification checklist for Gothic-style textiles
1. Is the pattern purely formal?
2. Is it symmetrical?
3. Is it derived from Gothic or medieval ornament?
4. Are there heraldic motifs?
5. Are the motifs clearly defined?
6. Are the leaves and flowers strictly conventionalized?

Early and High Victorian textiles
The classical style which prevailed during the Regency period gradually died out, to be replaced by a number of revived historical styles including Gothic, Elizabethan, Rococo (known at the time as Louis Quatorze) and the Moorish or Alhambresque.

Gothic style
This style was based mainly on the formal patterns of 15th and 16thC damasks and velvets, and its chief exponent was the architect, A. W. N. Pugin in the 1840s. The patterns usually have an ogival structure with stylized, scrolling leaves and heraldic motifs such as the fleur-de-lys, a style evident in the chalice veil in the main

picture. Pugin designed a number of ecclesiastical pieces for the new Gothic-inspired churches.

Pugin was a purist who believed in adhering strictly to authentic prototypes. He deplored the use of shaded architectural motifs, and the imitation of one material by another, such as printed chintz blinds designed to imitate a series of stained glass windows.

Rococo style
In the so-called "Louis Quatorze" style, Rococo scrolls and cartouches, shaded to give the appearance of relief, were incorporated into floral designs, notably for carpets.

Elizabethan style
This first appeared in about 1834, and became increasingly popular

in the 1840s and 50s. Some of the designs were purely abstract with bands of strapwork, cartouches and brackets. Others incorporated flowers with strapwork that was shaded to give a three-dimensional effect.

Moorish style

This type of pattern was inspired by Owen Jones's influential book, *Plans, Elevations, Sections and Details of the Alhambra* (1842). The intricate, interlaced patterns of delicately carved stonework, which operated on two or three intermingled planes, was copied in woven textiles, usually in primary colours. Geometric designs representing tilework are also found as well as vertical stripes of Moorish ornament introduced into floral patterns.

This woven silk textile, called *Maharanee*, was created by Owen Jones in c.1872. Jones was one of the finest designers of the Victorian period, and a leading promoter of flat pattern. He produced woven silks based on classical ornament, with anthemion and palmette motifs, Moorish designs, and patterns derived from Indian decoration, like this one.

Jones's celebrated *Grammar of Ornament* (1856) illustrated every known type of European ornament from prehistoric times to the Renaissance, together with examples from ancient Egypt, Assyria, Persia, India and China.

Traditional textiles

Among the most popular traditional types of the 1830s and 1840s were

silk damasks with formalized flowers and leaves in light colours. But these were luxury items and the more characteristic furnishing fabrics were power-loom woven in a mixture of cotton and worsted wool, or silk or wool, in darker colours.

This block-printed chintz with its crisply-drawn flowers on a white ground dates from 1835-40 and is typical of the early period. Machine-printed patterned grounds were also introduced at this time, the most popular being a simple all-over dot or pin design, known as a "Stormont" ground, or an all-over, vermicular pattern.

In the late 1840s, a continuous cascade of mixed flowers was printed vertically in the middle or on the sides of a fabric such as challet, a fine worsted woollen material with a distinct sheen, which enhanced the colours' brilliance. The patterns became more exuberant and naturalistic, using elaborate shading to make the flowers stand out from the ground. This style reached its peak in 1851, and was followed by more delicate patterns depicting ferns or heather.

Exotic styles

Used mainly in the cheaper, roller-printed fabrics, these included pictorial chintzes with a variety of romantic, historical and commemorative designs vignetted in floral wreaths. Textiles depicting incongruous groups of exotic flowers, animal and human figures were printed in bright colours on striped grounds. They were known as "Portuguese prints" and were intended for export to South America and elsewhere.

BERLIN WOOLWORK, SCREENS AND CROSSLEY MOSAICS

*A Berlin woolwork panel depicting a scene taken from
Sir Walter Scott's novel,* The Talisman
c.1840; ht 24in/61cm; value code E/F

Identification checklist for Berlin woolwork
1. Is the design worked in coloured wools (or silks)?
2. Is it worked on square-meshed canvas?
3. Is there one stitch to each square?
4. Is the squared effect apparent in the outline of the motifs?
5. Does the piece look like a picture?
6. Are the flowers naturalistically treated?

Berlin woolwork
This was the most popular type of
embroidery between the 1830s
and the 1870s, and was so-called
because the patterns and the
wools emanated from Berlin. The
designs were worked in wool,
sometimes with silk, in tent or
cross-stitch on square meshed
canvas, being copied from
patterns on squared paper. Many of
the designs were floral, depicting
roses, lilies-of-the-valley, poppies,
water-lilies and other popular
flowers, often combined with
exotic birds. The pictorial designs

included biblical subjects, designs
after Landseer or romantic
subjects taken from the novels of
Sir Walter Scott, like that shown
above. The panels were often
mounted in fire-screens or under
glass as table tops, and were also
used to upholster chair backs and
seats. Smaller items included
hand-screens and slipper tops.
   Parts of the pattern were
sometimes worked in a looped
stitch which was then cut to
resemble a velvet pile. Designs
were also worked wholly or partly
in glass beads.

Samplers

Berlin woolwork samplers were usually long narrow strips of canvas, bound in ribbon, worked with a variety of canvas stitches. Rectangular samplers, with the alphabet, a pious verse, and various other motifs, were also made throughout the Victorian period, more often worked in wool than silk.

This Berlin woolwork silk and wool sampler incorporates silver thread and beads in a variety of typical patterns including the Florentine stitch, imitation lace and three-dimensional effects.

Screens

From the 1870s, hand embroidery was often used to decorate three- and four-leaf screens, such as this one, designed by May Morris and produced by Morris and Company (see pp.154-5), who also produced a number of designs by J. H. Dearle.
* Many screen panels were produced by the Royal School of Needlework, founded in 1872, including designs by Selwyn Image (1840-1930) representing the Four Seasons and also figures of Greek and Roman goddesses.
* Japanese-inspired designs with water-plants, cranes and wildfowl with sprays of chyrsanthemum or *prunus* blossom were popular, and Liberty and other firms imported authentic examples of Japanese screens.

Crossley Mosaics

A purely Victorian innovation, Crossley Mosaics – velvet-like pictures and rugs, said to be the invention of a German refugee – were produced by John Crossley and Son of Halifax, between 1850 and 1869.

The designs, which were similar to those of Berlin woolwork, were worked out on squared paper. Threads of coloured worsted wool, one for each square of the pattern, were attached longitudinally to vertical frames, and by a complicated process cut into thin vertical slices and stuck to a linen backing, giving a depth of about $^3/_{10}$in (4mm). For rugs, the threads were backed onto a Brussels carpet to make them more durable.

As with Berlin woolwork, the subjects were often inspired by the paintings of Sir Edwin Landseer and others; Robbie Burns and Highland Mary shown *above*, were often depicted. As in other media, royalty were featured: there is a Crossley mosaic portrait of the Prince of Wales in a sailor suit.

PORTIÈRES, QUILTS AND SHAWLS

Detail of a Templeton portière designed by Bruce Talbert c.1878; length of whole piece 10ft/3.9m; value code F

Identification checklist for Templeton portières
1. Is the piece wool or silk?
2. Is it machine-woven?
3. Has the main area a repeating pattern?
4. Are the flowers stylized or conventional?
5. Are there bands of geometric ornament?
6. Does the piece show a Japanese influence?

Panels and portières
Textile hangings were especially popular during the Aesthetic period (see pp.10-11), when they were often used as curtains to cover doorways. One of the firms who specialized in these portières was James Templeton & Sons of Glasgow. Their wares were made of wool and silk woven on Jacquard looms, and designers included Bruce Talbert who created the piece illustrated in the main picture.

Templeton's wares often show a Japanese influence, with a broad border at the bottom, narrower borders at the sides, and a repeating pattern of flowers or ornament in the centre.

Other makers included the Royal School of Needlework, who produced embroidered designs, also with a Japanese flavour and featuring cranes, bamboo and *prunus* blossom, or the so-called

Jacobean "tree of life" pattern.

Morris & Co. (see pp.154-5) made hangings decorated with vine and acanthus leaves, flowering and fruiting trees and large floral sprays. These were designed by May Morris, J. H. Dearle or Morris himself.

Quilts
As in the United States (see pp.158-9), patchwork quilts were popular in Britain throughout the Victorian period. The traditional hexagonal patchwork quilts continued to be made throughout the Victorian period but often with scraps of silk and velvet instead of cotton. A type of patchwork known as *broderie perse* or Cretonne appliqué was made from about 1850 by sewing groups of flowers, birds and leaves cut from printed cotton onto a black ground.

"Box" patterns which simulated three-dimensional cubes, as in this mid-19thC quilt, were favoured, along with "log cabin" designs of oblong patches.

Appliqué and pieced quilts with repeated motifs in squared multiples, and patterns such as the *Star of Bethlehem*, were an American speciality, but similar examples were made in England. Another variety popular in the 1880s was "Japanese" or "crazy" patchwork – irregularly shaped, randomly arranged pieces, some with a flower or other motif, joined by featherstitch.

This detail from a "mosaic" patchwork hanging exemplifies a type that consisted of various coloured shapes cut from felt or tailors' cuttings and joined at the edges with almost invisible stitches. The designs were usually pictorial, with a strange mixture of religious and secular subjects derived from various sources such as popular prints and tinsel theatrical pictures.
* Other varieties included traditional, stitched quilts which consisted of two layers of fabrics with a blanket or padding between them. They were common in northern England and often had patterns of running feathers, cables, fans or bellows. "Strippy" or striped quilts were also popular in the North. These were decorated with full-length border patterns, or small rows of shells and roses. Quilts made in Wales usually had borders set in rectangular frames with a round centre, while West Country varieties featured a round centre with fan corners.

Shawls
The heyday of the shawl was in the 1850s and 60s when the ever-increasing width of crinoline made it difficult to wear a coat.

The earliest silk and wool shawls had a cream ground with a narrow, coloured border at the sides and a broad border at each end. Some were square with a plain or patterned centre of tiny stylized flowers or sprigs. Printed shawls made of fine muslin or gauze were preferred for summer wear.

"Paisley" shawls
The most popular type of shawl during the Victorian period was the so-called "Paisley" shawl, characterized by its use of a pine cone type of motif, of Kashmiri inspiration. Kashmiri-inspired shawls had been woven in Edinburgh and Norwich from the late 1770s, but were first woven in Paisley, Scotland, during the early 19thC and enjoyed a boom period there from the 1840s until the late 1860s.

The development of the Jacquard loom made it possible to manufacture Paisley shawls with complex all-over patterns in rich, dark colours (usually dominated by red). The example *above* is typical. They often had a central motif surrounded by scrolling patterns filled with Indian-inspired floral and leaf ornament, similar to that of this shawl, and broad borders depicting an elongated boteh (or pine-cone) pattern at each end.
* Similar designs were produced in Norwich and France at around the same period, so it is often difficult to make precise attributions.

LACE AND WHITEWORK

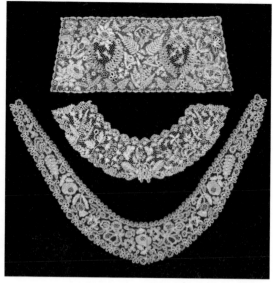

*Decorative collar and cuffs in Honiton lace
late 19thC; value code F*

Identification checklist for Honiton lace

1. Is the piece made from fine white cotton?
2. Has it naturalistic bobbin-made sprigs?
3. Are there roses, leaves, shells or butterflies with clear outlines?
4. Do any leaves have raised veins?
5. Is the ground a slightly irregular hexagonal mesh (this would indicate an earlier date)?
6. Is the ground a regular machine-made net?

Honiton lace

Honiton lace was the most sought-after British lace of the Victorian period, especially once it was chosen by Queen Victoria for her wedding veil and the flouncings and trimmings on her dress. A fine bobbin (or pillow) lace, the designs consist mainly of naturalistic sprays, mostly floral, although shells and butterflies often feature. The best examples include raised elements, worked in by "sewing in" threads into the existing pinholes, as in the veined leaves incorporated into the Honiton cuff and collars in the main picture. Typically, the motifs incorporated into these pieces are clearly outlined and fairly detailed. The whole is united by a net ground; this was initially hand-made, but from about 1825 machine net grounds were used increasingly.

Other bobbin lace

Although called Honiton lace, this type of bobbin lace was made all over Devon and also in the East Midlands. These patterns tend to be simpler, and were used mainly for trimmings, insertions and borders. Torchon lace, a coarse open-textured bobbin lace made in narrow lengths with geometric designs, was also produced in the East Midlands.

Nottingham lace

Nottingham lace-makers produced fine machine-made lace curtains with elaborate designs, as well as dress accessories. In the 1880s chemical lace was produced by embroidering fabric by machine, then dipping it into a chemical which dissolved the ground. These designs tended to be geometric and rather coarse.

Foreign lace

Imported Maltese lace, made with fairly coarse, often silk, thread with repeating patterns of stylized flowers and leaves, was much copied in England. Venetian lace, with its three-dimensional raised scrolling designs united by bars, was collected and copied by amateur lace-workers – lace-making being a popular pastime for gentlewomen of the late 19thC – often in ecru (a light brown colour achieved through the use of a dyed thread or by dipping the finished lace in tea).

Irish lace

Ireland produced a number of hand-made laces. Carrickmacross lace, introduced in 1816, was produced by applying fine cambric to machine-made net and adding embroidery stitches. Scrolling designs of flowers and leaves or delicate floral sprays were popular and the borders often have an edging of tiny loops. Limerick lace, introduced in 1829, was worked in stitches with a hook or needle on a machine net ground, usually with delicate floral designs. Crochet laces were an Irish speciality. The designs are usually floral with some of the petals standing free from the ground giving a three-dimensional effect. Pieces are often edged with little scalloped points.

Whitework

Whitework, a type of fine embroidery in white thread on muslin or fine cotton, was used in the making of dresses, christening robes, collars and cuffs, and so on. Pioneered by a Mrs Jameson of Ayrshire c.1814, it is also known as "Ayrshire" embroidery. More specialized was "Mountmellick" embroidery, which was usually worked on a white cotton satin jean in white knitting cotton, using satin stitch, chain and feather stitches and French knots to give a raised effect. Designs are naturalistic; often passion flowers, blackberries, ferns, oak leaves and

acorns. It was used to decorate bedspreads, pillow cases and costume, and although first popular in the 1850s, it enjoyed a revival in the 1880s when the leading publishers of needlework magazines, Weldon's, issued many patterns for it.

Patterns are mostly floral – for example roses, thistles, shamrocks, sprigs and leaves. The embroidered border *above* is a good example.

Broderie anglaise

By c.1850, *broderie anglaise* (also known from the 1880s as "Madeira work") began to replace Ayrshire work in popularity. Designs tended to be either geometric or very conventionalized flowers and leaves, and consisted of a series of cut holes worked round in buttonhole stitch. The patterns *above*, for *broderie anglaise* show the looped and scalloped edges typical of this type of work. These designs come from a contemporary embroidery manual; many such instruction books were published in the late 19thC for the amateur lace-maker and embroiderer.

THE AESTHETIC
MOVEMENT

Dragonfly, *part of a woven silk tissue by Bruce Talbert c.1875; value code for a sample F/G, for a curtain D/E.*

Identification checklist for "Aesthetic" period textiles
1. Does the design incorporate conventionalized flowers, with flat petals, possibly sunflowers or lilies?
2. Are the colours subdued, usually olive and grey-green, or pale turquoise?
2. Does the design feature any *prunus* or apple blossom?
4. Is there any fruit, particularly pomegranates?
5. Is a Japanese influence evident?

The Aesthetic Movement
The Aesthetic Movement of the 1870s and 1880s was a self-conscious revival of the decorative arts. One of the main influences was the art of Japan, which affected not only painting but all the applied arts, including textiles, and which can be seen in the designs by any of those prominent in the Movement. Other inspiration came from classical, Medieval and Renaissance art.

Colours
Most of the Aesthetic textiles, whether woven or printed, are in subdued colours such as soft olive and grey-greens, satirized by Gilbert and Sullivan as "greenery-yallery", or blue-green and pale turquoise. Others, notably some designed by Dresser and Talbert, are in red and gold on a black background, simulating the effect of Japanese lacquer.

The Aesthetic Gallery in Old Bond Street, London, was established c.1890 and specialized in artistic silken fabrics of English manufacture. This late 1880s velveteen with pomegranates, printed by Thomas Wardle, is a typical example.

Edwin William Godwin (English, 1833-86)

The sketchbooks of the architect E. W. Godwin (see pp.22-3) are filled with drawings of Japanese badges and ornaments, elements of which he included in the textiles he designed for Warner and Sons in the early 1870s. His were some of the finest textiles of the Aesthetic period.

Some of Godwin's designs have a rigid geometrical structure,

enclosing highly conventionalized flowers reduced to a flat, circular form, against a background of Japanese ornament. In the example *above*, this treatment has been applied to sunflowers, one of his most typical motifs. The stiff leaves display a medieval influence. His textiles and wallpapers also include peacocks, kingfishers and sparrows treated in a Japanese manner.

Bruce Talbert (English, 1838-81)

Even more prolific and influential as a textile designer was Bruce Talbert (see also pp.20-1), whose designs are somewhat similar to those of Godwin. Many of his textiles, which include stamped velvet as well as woven silks and printed cottons, are all-over patterns of leaves and blossom, the flowers being conventionalized shapes with flat petals.

The *Dragonfly* design in the main picture, a woven silk tissue, shows dragonflies hidden amongst an all-over pattern of peach-blossom, leaves and fruit. Like Godwin, Talbert favoured sunflowers, sometimes stylized, sometimes drawn with an almost botanical accuracy. Oscar Wilde regarded the sunflower and the lily as "the two most perfect models of design, the most naturally adapted for decorative art" and, together with peacock's feathers, they were practically the symbols of the Aesthetic movement.

Other Aesthetic designers

Christopher Dresser designed a number of textiles; some display stylized floral motifs set in a rigid geometric structure, whilst others are clearly modelled on the Japanese. Other textile designers of the Aesthetic Movement were Walter Crane and Lewis F. Day. The textile designs of William Morris also belong to the Aesthetic period but are discussed in a separate section (see pp.154-5).

The embroidery of the period was known as "art needlework" and became as much of a craze as the Berlin woolwork that preceded it (see pp.146-7). Much of the embroidery was floral, the favourite motifs being sunflowers, lilies, daffodils, iris, tulips, daisies, primroses and wild roses, together with *prunus* and apple blossom and sprays of chrysanthemum. The example *above*, a detail from a design by E. D. Bradby, shows an exquisitely embroidered white lily.
* Embroidery was used to adorn table covers and cloths, mats and doilies, sideboard cloths, chair backs, mantel borders and fire-screens. Curtains, bedspreads, piano covers and hangings provided great scope for the ambitious art needlewoman and were worked on linen and cotton twill, serge and velvet, often in crewel wools.

Other Aesthetic motifs

Renaissance-type patterns with dolphins, grotesque beasts, *putti* and scrollwork were also favoured, particularly by Walter Crane, as well as designs based on Turkish, Persian, and Cretan embroideries. Patterns for embroidery were published by the Royal School of Art Needlework and other organizations. Figure panels from the Aesthetic period, notably those by Selwyn Image, were depicted in classical or medieval dress, worked either in outline, in shades of brown, or in appliqué.

MORRIS & CO.

Detail from a William Morris Hammersmith runner
c.1882; 98 x 41ft/38.5 x16m; value code A

Identification checklist for Morris Hammersmith
carpets and rugs
1. Is the piece hand-knotted?
2. Has it approximately 25 knots to the square inch?
3. Has it a deep pile?
4. Are the knots of pure wool?
5. Are the colours "soft" indicating vegetable dyes?
6. Are the floral motifs stylized?
7. Are the motifs outlined in a contrasting colour?
8. Does the design show the influence of Persian carpets?
9. Is there a mark of a hammer and "M"? (This is found
only on early examples.)

Morris & Co. (English, 1861-1940, initially as Morris, Marshall, Faulkner & Co. until 1875)
The poet, writer, socialist and designer, William Morris, is chiefly remembered today for his textiles and wallpapers. His firm was founded in 1861 to produce a variety of products including furniture (see pp.24-5) and changed its name to Morris and Company in 1875. Morris designed his first textile, *The Jasmine Trellis*, in 1868.

In all, Morris created over 50 designs for printed and woven textiles, together with designs for embroideries, carpets and tapestries. They were usually printed by hand from wood-blocks using vegetable dyes, such as madder, weld and indigo, which look pleasant even when faded.

Nearly all of Morris's designs depict stylized but recognizable flowers which retain a feeling of living growth within a historic pattern structure. Birds are often incorporated as well.

Reproductions

Many of Morris's patterns have been reproduced, among them wallpaper designs made as fabrics, or adapted to a smaller scale. These are all screen- or machine-printed in modern, chemical dyes which look more uniform than the vegetable colours of the originals (see *below*).

The pattern of this printed cotton textile, *The Strawberry Thief*, was designed by Morris in 1883. This piece was printed by the indigo discharge method whereby a bleach is used to remove the blue dye, leaving traces on the reverse. In modern reproductions, printed using modern chemical dyes, this does not occur.
* Other examples of indigo discharge Morris textiles include the *Wey* and the *Wandle*.

Carpets

In the 1870s, Morris made a number of designs for machine-made carpets and in 1880 he set up carpet looms in Hammersmith to produce hand-knotted rugs influenced by Persian and other Eastern carpets. In 1881, the looms were moved to his Merton Abbey Workshops. The hand-knotted carpets were expensive, but of such high quality that many have survived. The detail in the main picture shows part of a runner made for the London house of the Greek Consul's son.

Other textiles

Other textiles produced by Morris & Co. include:
* portières (curtains intended to be hung in a doorway)
* wall hangings
* cushion covers
* firescreen panels
* three-panelled embroidered screens
* pure silk damasks
* heavy worsted woollen fabrics (often with a twill weave), such as *Peacock* and *Dragon*. Modern reproductions are often woven in synthetic or mixed fibres.

Embroideries

In the 1860s and 70s, Morris produced designs for church embroidery, for the Royal School of Needlework, and for individual houses, but most extant examples date from after 1885, when Morris's daughter, May, took charge of the firm's embroidery section, producing, together with Morris's chief assistant, J. H. Dearle, finished embroideries and designs traced out for the customers to work themselves. Patterns by May and Dearle were mainly floral (often depicting poppies) and looser than William's.

This tapestry of *Flora* was woven in 1881. Morris designed few complete tapestries and usually concentrated on backgrounds and borders. Figures were provided by the painter Edward Burne-Jones. The background of *Flora* was supplied by J. H. Dearle, but Morris was responsible for the original design in a larger format, which had a background of acanthus leaves. Dearle's backgrounds are generally stiffer and coarser than Morris's and lack their complexity.

LIBERTY & CO.

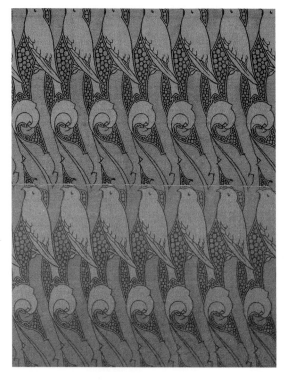

Birds and Berries, *a silk and wool reversible double-cloth designed by C. F. A. Voysey for
Liberty & Co.
c.1897; 104 x 46in/264 x 117cm;
value code: for a sample G, for a pair of curtains F.*

Identification checklist for textiles by C. F. A. Voysey
1. Is the design based on natural forms?
2. Are leaves and flowers stylized?
3. Are motifs clearly defined or outlined?
4. Are colours flat with no hint of shading?
5. If any birds or animals, are these reduced to a flat
silhouette?
6. Does the design include flowing curves?

**Liberty and Co. (England,
1875-present)**
Since its foundation, Liberty has
been famous for its textiles. The
earliest were silks imported from
the East, either plain or printed
with Indian- or Japanese-inspired
designs. In the 1880s the firm
introduced its "Art Fabrics",
which were innovative in their
inclusion of English-style Art
Nouveau elements into Aesthetic
designs. The firm commissioned
work from leading artists of the
day, including Christopher
Dresser, Walter Crane, Lindsay
Butterfield and C. F. A. Voysey
(see pp.28-9).

Typical features

The sinuous, undulating lines of Voysey's designs, evident in *Birds and Berries*, in the main picture, are typical of his fabrics and of Liberty prints in the last decade of the 19thC, which were to prove very influential in the development of the Art Nouveau style on the Continent. The stylized effect is partly achieved by the precision with which the pattern is drawn, further emphasized by a heavy outline. Typically, the colours are flat and the application unrelieved by shading.

* Birds in flight or perched on branches were recurring Voysey motifs. Birds drawn by William Morris (see pp.154-5) are more realistic with coloured flecks used to indicate the feathers.

* Designs by Lindsay Butterfield show the influence of both Morris and Voysey, and are predominantly floral, with poppies, iris, daffodils and lilies among his favourite plants. These tend to be drawn with greater botanical accuracy than those of Voysey, and are instantly recognizable.

Lotus

Most of the Liberty designs are floral: especially popular are those with poppies, anemones, irises, tulips, or, as in the example *above*, lotus flowers. Scrolling acanthus-like leaves are also popular.

Original or reproduction?

Liberty designs were originally intended as furnishing fabrics. However, in the 1960s many designs were revived for dresses and scarves, and some are still in production today. These are usually printed on silk or wool, whereas the original designs were printed on cotton or velveteen, or woven as silk and wool double cloths or so-called "tapestries"

Silver Studio

A number of designs were produced for Liberty by the Silver Studio during the 1890s. Those by Arthur Silver tend to display swirling, sinuous lines, often with a marked discrepancy of scale.

From c.1900, Liberty designs, including some by Harry Napper, another Silver Studio designer, became more formal and stiffer. These tended to display Glasgow-style roses – more or less circular roses with stylized, elliptical rings, as in the example, *above*. Spade- or heart-shaped leaves, formalized trees or berries and grapes with squared-up leaves were also popular, with plain grounds rather than the densely patterned ones of their earlier designs.

Attribution

Although Liberty had its own print-works at Merton Abbey, the textiles were usually produced by outside firms, and most of the designers – who were not credited by Liberty – also worked for other companies. However, it is still possible to find examples of Victorian Liberty fabrics which bear the original maker's label, as does the *Lotus* design.

The British Silk Association

Liberty took a prominent part in the setting up in 1887 of the British Silk Association, in an attempt to revive the hand-woven Spitalfields silks and machine-woven silks from Macclesfield, which were facing increased foreign competition. Among the Spitalfields silks commissioned by Liberty in 1891 was a design of honeysuckle and jasmine, and of *Iris* on a fish-scale background. Less expensive fabrics commissioned from Macclesfield included a *Hop and Ribbon* silk damask, registered in 1892, and *Cascade,* inspired by falling water.

AMERICAN QUILTS

An Album-type appliqué cotton quilt
late 19thC; 91x76in/218.5x182.5cm; value code C/D

Identification checklist for American patchwork quilts
1. Is the item hand-made?
2. Is the stitching and other needlework exemplary?
3. Is it stitched in a decorative or diamond pattern?
4. Does the quilt contain several needlework techniques?
5. Are the motifs or pattern arrangements uniquely American in origin?
6. Is the piece bold and brightly coloured?
7. Do the motifs recall rustic motifs or folk art, or are the panels arranged in a random order like crazy-paving?

American quilts

American quilt-making came into its own at the start of the 19thC. Most examples seen on today's market were made between then and the 1930s.

Patchwork quilts were originally made up from scraps of left-over fabrics to save money when textiles were very expensive. The craft was especially popular in rural settlements and some of the best pieces were made by women in the mid-Atlantic states such as Maryland and the Carolinas.

Superbly-crafted quilts were also

made by the German-speaking communities of the northeast, such as the Mennonites, the Amish and the so-called Pennsylvania Dutch, and these examples preserve traditional European designs and techniques. Pennsylvania Dutch quilts are typically boldly coloured and patterned in a style that evokes central European folk art.

In many cases, the coverlets were the work of more than one person, and they were often made as presentation pieces for special occasions such as weddings and births. In some areas, unmarried girls were expected to produce thirteen quilts for their dowries.

The techniques include patchwork or appliqué, embroidery and stencilling, but there are examples where the quilt stitching alone forms the decoration.

American quilts can be categorized according to their pattern, technique and region of origin. Their value today rests on the skills and inventiveness of the needlewomen who made them, usually without a sewing machine.

Patterns

American quilts were often given picturesque pattern names. Perhaps the most well-known design to have evolved in the mid-19thC is the "log cabin". This type was a pieced quilt, rustic in flavour and usually composed of identical small, square blocks arranged with a diagonal emphasis. The stitching technique involved anchoring the squares to a base fabric. Log cabin quilts were often made from inexpensive cotton or wool, but examples tend to be small.

The "Album" (or "albumen") pattern, illustrated in the main picture, was also popular in the mid-19thC. These are the work of several women, often from a religious community or an extended family, each of whom would produce a small, square panel. When these had been stitched together, the piece was finally sewn to a fabric ground. Sometimes the individual makers signed and dated their panels.
* Quilt patterns took on a new lease of life during Centennial year. From this date, designs often featured symbols of the American Republic, such as the stars and stripes and the Imperial eagle.
* Among the finest of all American quilts were those that imitated delicate Italian *trapunto* patterns. The technique relies solely on the

stitching for its decorative effect, and is carried out on a monochrome ground.
* As in other areas of American crafts during 1876, Japanese art also made an impact on quilt-making, although examples are very rare.

"Crazy quilts" also date from the 1870s and 1880s. As illustrated in the example shown *above*, they were made from odd scraps of fabric (usually silk or elaborately printed) cut and arranged at random. This piece incorporates a souvenir ribbon from a New Orleans exposition of 1884. The resulting effect is made more "crazy" by a variety of stitching techniques.

Crazy quilts were particularly fashionable in the late 1880s when people could buy the components in kit form. The most popular examples are those which combine a high standard of needlework with imaginative compositions.

This "hooked" wool rug shows another popular collecting area of American textiles. Most were made in the English cottage tradition throughout the Victorian period. Those in good condition and depicting American images are the most valuable today. This example probably came from New Hampshire in c.1885.

MISCELLANEOUS

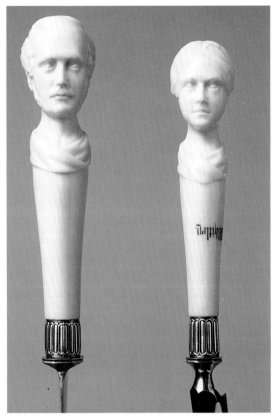

*A knife and fork with ivory handles carved with the busts of
Queen Victoria and Prince Albert*

The Victorians were great accumulators: every available wall
and surface of the late 19thC home was covered with a
proliferation of paraphernalia, some of it functional, some
decorative and some completely useless.

A large number of decorative objects were commercially
produced, but many of those pieces that survive today (even
some of the most accomplished) were the work of amateurs –
for example, hand-painted china, portraits and miniatures.

The Victorians had a passion for disguising objects; not
even the most everyday things were allowed to be simply what
they were. Doorstops took the form of all manner of creatures
– for example, bowls were veined to resemble leaves and
menu holders were fashioned to look like walnuts on a stem.

It was an age of great experimentation in decoration and
materials – for example, objects, such as crucifixion groups,

were fashioned out of bread, sugar and coal. Sadly, few of these have survived. Crucifixion groups were also made in bottles, as were ships. Glass-domed table displays of simulated flowers constructed from ornate compositions of shells, feathers, silk or wax (see pp. 164-5) were popular. Stuffed animals and birds also graced the living or dining room. Although usually displayed in a naturalistic setting, they were sometimes arranged in novelty form. Somewhat perversely, there was a renewed fashion for wood carvings representing dead animals and bird, usually game. Living birds in elaborate cages were also a popular novelty in the Victorian drawing room.

As the reign progressed and photography became a more affordable and widespread hobby, mantelpieces increasingly displayed the results, first with daguerreotypes and later, photographs, some enhanced by a colour tint.

The Victorian fashion for the seaside holiday, and the great expansion of the travel industry, led to a craze for holiday souvenirs. Pieces from English holiday resorts tended to feature the ubiquitous shellwork, or involved glazed pictures made of local sand, often layered in different tones, or made entirely from seaweed. Souvenir tablewares, particularly plates and cups, were also popular. Souvenirs from more exotic places tended to be indigenous or tribal objects, often given a practical use. For example, elephant feet were hollowed out and used as umbrella stands, or stuffed and used for seating. The taste for the Oriental in Britain and the United States during the second half of the 19thC led to the increasing popularity of bamboo, both as a decorative motif and for furniture and other objects.

The importance of the kitchen in the household reached unprecedented proportions during Victoria's reign. Coupled with the spirit of technical advancement and invention, this led to the patenting of a vast range of newfangled kitchen aids, including apple corers, marmalade cutters, butter makers, copper and porcelain jelly moulds, and every conceivable iron. All are very collectable today.

Ephemera of the period is also sought-after, from Christmas and Valentine cards, to souvenirs of important events. Any item connected with death – the great Victorian preoc-cupation – are surprisingly collectable (see pp. 166-7).

During the 19thC, a greater variety of toys and dolls were available than ever before: for the first time, dolls could walk, talk, cry and even swim. Toys, which had previously been made only in wood, were now produced in the United States in tinplate and in Germany and elsewhere in cast iron. Many had brightly painted, and later, lithographed, bodies. A few had clockwork motors.

The scope for the collector of Victorian miscellany is vast and there is still a great potential for making a good investment. From the evidence so far, it seems that no item, however trivial, should be overlooked.

DOLLS

The second half of the 19thC saw a huge increase in doll manufacture throughout Europe. The wooden dolls of the 18thC gave way to examples made from papier-mâché, wax, composition (tough combinations of wood pulp and paper), cloth and china. German doll-makers were the most prolific, although French examples are considered the best, especially those with bisque faces. Some are marked, often on the back of the neck or shoulder plate, with the name or trademark of the maker and other information such as the mould number.

Wax dolls

Wax dolls, and those with a composition head covered with wax were made in France, Germany and England. They are prone to cracking, but are extremely desirable if in good condition. "Character" dolls, with original and realistic (rather than idealized) expressions, are particularly sought after. The example *above*, is a rare crying baby doll from c.1870, by John Edwards, a renowned British maker. Most dolls of this era were miniature adults; babies and children were not made in great numbers until c.1900.

Bisque dolls

The best bisque (unglazed china) dolls were produced by two Parisian factories, Bru Jeune and Jumeau. The example *above*, made by Jumeau, is a portrait doll (the term for early Jumeau dolls), and was intended to represent a particular person, if only loosely. This example features sought-after paperweight eyes (made of blown glass), particularly common on French dolls.
* Many bisque dolls known as "fashion dolls" or "Parisiennes" represent a woman or adolescent with well-finished, fashionable clothes, which are often detailed copies of contemporary fashions. The value of fashion dolls depends on the condition of the bisque heads and on whether hair and clothes are original. The doll above has her original wooden and kid body, real hair, satin dress and kid shoes and is consequently particularly valuable.
* Collectors should keep a note of any alterations made after purchase – for example, to clothing.

Automata

Automata (mechanical dolls and toys) were manufactured in quantity between 1880 and 1920. This early French example has a bisque head and hands and a mechanical key-wound body. The first time the girl hits the box with her magic wand (missing on this example) nothing happens. The second time, a head pops up.

TOYS

The range of available toys was not great until the end of the 19thC and mostly consisted of lead soldiers known as "flats", and wooden toys, especially skittles, miniature shops and Noah's arks complete with animals. Tin toys were made in the United States from the 1830s but not in any quantity in Europe until the end of the 19thC.

Wooden toys

The wooden rocking horse was probably the most popular toy of the Victorian period. This example is late Victorian and in very good condition. Even those with a small amount of damage, such as a missing eye, are collectable.
* European toys are usually carved or turned, with the decoration painted directly on to the wood; American pieces are flat and covered with lithographed paper.

Cast-iron toys

Most cast-iron novelty money boxes were made in the United States, where they were very popular. This *Girl Skipping Rope* is a desirable example designed by James H. Bowen and made by J. & E. Stevens of Cromwell,

Connecticut in 1890. Depression of a small lever causes the girl to skip over the rope.
* Being brittle, cast-iron tends to snap easily and, as it is difficult to repair intact examples, and those with original paint command a premium.
* Reproductions, which abound, lack the fine detail and depth of colour of the originals.

Tin toys

Tin toys (made of tinplated steel) were produced in many forms including animals, cars and boats. The Americans led the way in the 1830s; production did not take place in Europe on a large scale until toward the end of the 19thC.

The Germans were among the first European companies to produce tin toys. This German soldier and sentry box, made c.1890, and the mounted soldier, were probably part of a larger set of soldiers, horses and guards.
* The best-known German maker was Ernst Paul Lehmann, many of whose toys carry printed patent dates. Some pieces include flywheel-operated movements.
* Tin toys made before c.1890 are hand-painted; later examples are printed. Sometimes, an early painted toy was reproduced using printed parts.
* Condition is all-important with this category of toys as they are prone to rusting and denting. Painted surfaces are vulnerable to chipping or flaking; printed finishes are easily scratched or rubbed. Restoration is sometimes possible but can halve a toy's value.

Value point
Many Victorian toys are fetching unprecedented prices, but some can still be bought inexpensively, especially games, jigsaws and educational toys. Automata can fetch very high prices today, even those that are not in perfect condition.

TABLE DISPLAYS

Table displays of imitation flowers, stuffed birds or miniature figures covered by a glass dome were among the most popular forms of decoration in the 19thC drawing room or parlour. Known by the Victorians as "shades" because of their glass coverings, many were designed to be seen from all sides and could stand on a table in the middle of the room or on top of a mantelpiece. The arrangements were often extremely ornate, highly realistic and usually involved a great deal of skill and ingenuity.

A variety of media were used to form displays, including fabric, shell, wax, glass, feathers and even human hair.

Wax figures under glass domes were also popular and include religious figures (especially of the Madonna and Child, made for Roman Catholic households), domestic scenes and sentimental representations of children and animals.

The basket of imitation rosebuds, *below*, is made from stained cockleshells mounted on wires and stuck into a moss base. The leaves are of dyed and glazed cotton, and the heart of each rose is represented by a winkle – a novel treatment of a fairly common theme.

This display, *below*, illustrates one of the ingenious methods used by the Victorians to reproduce flowers and leaves. At first glance, the petals and foliage look as though they have been made from fabric, but in fact they are feathers that have been carefully shaped and wired together.

* Although many displays are anonymous, some domes bear a paper label with the retailer's name.

Although baskets containing glass or wax fruit, or glass fruit coated in wax, were popular, currants and grapes, like those depicted *below* are uncommon subjects. This arrangement is all the more unusual in showing only one type of fruit. The grapes are made of glass dipped in coloured wax. As

can be seen from the detail, the wax is prone to peeling, or to forming a mouldy bloom. The fruit can be treated using a buttered pastry knife; such work is probably best left to a professional restorer.

* Typically, the basket is made of wirework dipped in wax. The base is ebonized wood (in keeping with much of the furniture of the day).
* The dome is too high for the group and is probably not original: an original dome will be in proportion to the display, which should fill all the available space.

This shade of stuffed birds, *right*, is among the most elaborate of its type. The wooden base is carved around the rim. Not untypically, the colours of the birds' breast feathers have been "touched up" to make them look more brilliant than they really were. The most popular versions included exotic birds, such as humming birds.

Note
The thin and brittle glass domes are extremely fragile and are often replaced. Victorian glass has air bubbles and imperfections – not features of modern glass.

Shell displays were extremely labour-intensive and are regarded as being among the most desirable of all Victorian shades. This example, *left*, is particularly elaborate and realistic, and depicts several different varieties of flower on an imitation rockwork base, also made of shells.
* Shell and shell fragments were popular items of decoration throughout the 19thC; the shells were collected in Great Britain and imported from around the Empire. Large quantities of mother-of-pearl were imported from the Channel Islands to Birmingham to be used as inlay in papier-mâché furniture (see pp.14-15).

FUNERALIA

The Victorian age is often remembered as the great age of mourning. Several factors contributed to an increasing obsession with death, including the high mortality rate, and a growing dissatisfaction with the terrible burial conditions, which resulted in a demand for permanent protected burial grounds. In addition, the country had seen several State funerals – in particular that of Prince Albert, and the Duke of Wellington – which set a precedent for lavish burials. The Queen was in deep mourning and her subjects emulated her. The rules of protocol were strict, with codes of conduct not only for the funeral itself but also for the clothes and belongings of the bereaved. Nothing, however trivial, was exempt from being "funeralized": even parasols, ear trumpets, fans and crockery were black or adorned with the motifs commonly associated with mourning – for example, arum lillies.

Although many mourning items have gone the way of all flesh, there is still a fair number on the market – for example, mourning cards undertakers' bills and other funeral paraphernalia, mourning crockery and so on. Currently, they are not highly sought-after but, as with all items of historical

interest, there is a market for them and prices may be set to rise over the next few years.

Known as "immortals", flower arrangements like that shown *above*, were intended to stand on a grave or to be hung above a vault – the fittings usually allowed them to be used in either way. This example, typically, is made of plaster over tin. Immortals were made into the early years of this century, but few have survived. The flowers are invariably white for purity. Other motifs include doves and clasped hands.

Mourning paraphernalia associated with the Royal Family commands a premium. The set *below* includes an announcement of the Queen's death, and black-edged royal stationery.

Mourning cards were often ordered by the undertaker on behalf of the bereaved. Some were sent as notifications of the death, others as invitations to the funeral or simply in remembrance of the deceased. The "In Memoriam" card developed out of the embossed and pierced examples produced earlier in the century. Many, especially those from later in the period, were

Death was also commemorated in needlework and samplers, often executed by children. This Berlin woolwork sampler (see pp.146-7) is headed "In Affectionate Remembrance of Ellen Walker Who died December 5th 1853 Aged 69." The three verses are framed by symbols associated with death: the broken column is symbolic of life cut short, while the fountain represents life itself. Willows were commonly used to suggest tears.
* All Victorian samplers should be dated: this example has the name and date stitched into the bottom, underneath the tomb, and reads "Mary Ann Howarth Aged 12 1854".

pictorial, like that shown *above left*. The wreath, *above right*, was another typical motif. The card commemorating the death of James Renforth (*above bottom*) in a rowing accident in 1871 is particularly desirable as it has a "story" and gives an account of how the death occurred.
* Mourning cards are worth more if they retain their original black-edged envelope. Even undertakers' bills are collectable.

For the wealthy at least, the funeral was a lavish affair, with every detail made to reflect the solemnity of the occasion – even the horses pulling the hearse wore black feather plumes, a few of which have survived and are collectable. Many coffins were adorned with pressed tin coffin plates like that shown *left*, although, like most of those found today, it was never actually used on a coffin. They have not survived in number. The subject and size determine the religion, sex and age of the deceased – for example, pale blue was used for children or infants, black for adults. White was usual for girls, especially virgins (unmarried women). This coffin plate depicts an angel with a trumpet held on high and is of a type often manufactured in Birmingham or Wolverhampton.

VALENTINE CARDS

Some cards had elaborate cut-out borders, such as the example shown, *left*, and some examples combine these with other elaborate embellishment such as embossing or pierced work. Many were even scented – for example, with patchouli.

The very late Victorian valentine card pictured *below* was made c.1900. The stylized, stem-like design around the girl's feet shows the influence of Continental Art Nouveau, while the costume worn by the girl is unmistakeably Victorian.

The custom of sending valentine cards originated in the late 18thC, reached its height in the Victorian age, and died out towards the end of the century when it was superseded by the market for Christmas cards. Its present-day revival dates from the end of the Second World War.

The first examples were hand-written and -painted, but cards with etched or lithographed outlines, sometimes left blank for the senders to fill in themselves, came into fashion soon afterwards. The most characteristic varieties, elaborately decorated with ribbon bows, pressed flowers, shells or metal hearts, were made from the late 1840s. Messages ranged from the simple "Be my valentine" to verses of four lines or more, usually containing elaborate promises of undying love. However, toward the end of the century, many cards began to be more light-hearted and their messages more humorous. The message was often concealed on a small card inserted beneath a flap on the front of the valentine.

Cards bordered with gold-coloured bronze powder were popular in the 1840s, and from the mid-19thC, people often sent novelty cards, such as "flower-cage" valentines.

Even some top designers turned their attention to decorating valentine cards – for example, Walter Crane. Such cards, where they can be attributed, command a premium.

Pictorial cards that feature contemporary inventions such as the typewriter depicted here, or contemporary dress, were especially popular towards the end of the 19thC.
* Cherubs were popular subjects on valentines throughout the 19thC.

Among the rarest Victorian valentines are imitation banknotes, telegrams and postal orders.

Another late 19thC refinement was the pull-up card, which was sent on Valentine's Day and at Christmas time. This card of a girl in a flower cart is a typical example: the cart and girl fold flat onto the card base.
* Other novelty cards include those with moving limbs, held together by tabs and operated by a lever.

Sailors' valentines
"Sailors' valentines" were traditionally not cards but octagonal, wooden boxes – smooth, polished wood for officers, cheaper cedar for ordinary seamen. They were made singly or in hinged pairs, decorated with shells arranged in mosaic patterns under a glass cover. There was usually a five-pointed star, an anchor or other nautical device at the centre. Underneath, a message such as "Truly thine" or "Forget-me-not" was picked out in shells.

Pierced paper lace, silver embossed paper cutouts and three-dimensional flower designs contribute to the very elaborate feel of this cameo card, *below*. The clothes of the two figures identify it as late-Victorian.

Applied decoration on cards was often very inventive and made use of a variety of materials. This elaborate card, *below*, is decorated with dried leaves as well as the more usual paper lace and embossed work. It was made between 1860 and 90, possibly by Rimmel, one of the best-known makers.
* Some cards in this style also include printed verses.

This cameo-embossed card, *below*, is decorated with a pierced paper lace border characteristic of the early to mid-Victorian period. The central motif is colour-printed using chromolithography and surrounded by a printed verse on a raised ground. One of the most prolific manufacturers of these types of card was H. Dobbs, "Ornamental Stationer" to the Royal Family.
* A few cards carry a printed maker's mark on the back.

PHOTOGRAPHIC IMAGES

Until the middle of the 19thC the only form of portable image was the miniature portrait. These remained popular throughout the Victorian period, but were progressively replaced by the daguerreotype, the precursor of the modern photograph.

Daguerreotypes

French-born Louis Daguerre (1787-1851) did not invent photography, but he refined the existing process and, crucially, developed the means of permanently fixing an image onto a surface. Images created using this process, called daguerreotypes, were the first form of photography to be made generally available and were first seen in the 1840s. The earliest examples tend to be small. They are extremely delicate and generally kept behind sealed glass – they need to be well treated to survive. The most common subjects are portraits and family groups, although topographical studies and still lives also exist. Candid photographs were also taken, and there appears to have been a trade in erotic and art studies.

* Condition – of both the image and the cover – is all-important. Restoration is extremely difficult and must be left to a professional.
* Daguerreotypes still represent good value for money, but interesting compositions are always expensive, especially when details of the sitters are recorded.
* Collectors should beware of images "married" to the wrong case. The image should be a good fit and look as if it has always been with the case.
* In the United States any Civil War subject is sought-after.

Some daguerreotypes, such as the example shown *above*, from a ladies' travelling case, were tinted in order to give a more lifelike appearance. Although this tinted portrait is conventionally mounted, many others had bakelite cases.

Daguerreotypes were framed in a variety of ways. This example has a hand-painted paper case. Made in the United States, it bears a label "Meade & Brothers", who may have been the case-makers rather than the photographers.

Ambrotypes

The ambrotype process was the result of exposing a glass plate treated with the wet collodion chemical process. The resulting negative image was made positive by placing black paper behind the glass plate — the ambrotype. The ambrotype thus comprises outer case, clear glass dust cover, metal mount, glass ambrotype plate and black backing. Ambrotypes are more commonly found today than dageurreotypes, but are not as popular with collectors.

* Ambrotype is am American term, not always used in Britain in the 19thC.
* Daguerreotypes have a metallic copperish sheen when held in a certain light. Ambrotypes are mounted on a glass plate. Daguerreotypes are less liable to disintegrate than ambrotypes, as the collodion chemical used in the ambrotype process can flake.

This group of three women have the typically uncomfortable and stilted poses often found on early ambrotypes: in order to get a clear image the subject's head was held from behind throughout the period of exposure (usually about twenty seconds) in order to keep it absolutely still.

Stereoscopic viewers
Both daguerreotypes and ambrotypes could also be adapted by duplication for stereoscopic viewers. However, the equipment was prohibitively expensive until late in the century, when a New York-based company called Underwood and Underwood developed an inexpensive hand-held viewer. Many cards were produced, covering a variety of subjects including topographical, ethnographical and military. They were housed in cases fashioned as two cards joined by a spine, which was embossed with the subject matter.

Hand-held viewers, like that shown *above*, are collectable in their own right. This example originally had a thin felt lipping where the edge rested against the face. Almost all the popular contemporary photographs were available in stereoscopic form.

Cartes de visite
The ambrotype eventually gave way to the laying of an image on paper or card. Several "copies" could be taken from one exposure, so customers were offered several photographs of the same subject, resulting in a mania for swapping and sending *cartes de visite* to friends and relations. The mounting of an image on card also led to the general availability of photographs for sale in shops; favourite topics included the Royal Family, topographical views, and architectural studies.

With the popularity of the photograph came the fashion for photograph albums. Examples can be found today, with or without photographs, bound in leather, ivory, silver or, very occasionally, gold. Some are bound in mauchline, which is printed sycamore wood. The example *above*, is of leather and mother-of-pearl. Some of the more expensive examples tend to have been purpose-made for a specific series of photographs, whilst some examples contain collections of *cartes de visite*. Price will depend not only on the elaborateness of the decoration of the album, but also on whether there is an identifying inscription or dedication plaque (as on the example pictured here). Should the album contain photographs or *cartes de visite*, its value will be dictated by their quality and condition.

Towards the end of the century miniature photographs began to replace the painted miniature (or more rarely, hair) as the popular insert for the locket (see p. 116).

Many were tinted. However, the anonymity of the vast majority of these portraits means that most are of small, if any value.

The advent of the Kodak Brownie roll film camera in the 1890s resulted in more people taking their own photographs, and the fall of the studio phogographer (except society photographers) dates from this time.

SCRAPWORK AND DECALCOMANIA

Scrapwork
Scraps were also used to adorn screens. At first, they were taken from magazines, but later they were manufactured specially and sold by craft shops.

The subjects represented are diverse and tend to be typically Victorian. Heroes of the Empire were common, as well as children, animals, and well known pictures of the day. All aspects of idyllic rustic, domestic and military life were represented – the detail from an oak-framed scrapscreen, *above*, displays a typical hotch-potch. Some screens are thematic, for example, representing the seasons. Scrapwork was as popular in Germany and the United States as in Britain. Indeed, Raphael Tuck, the most famous manufacturer of scraps, was based in Germany and New York. Some screens bear the printed name of the scrap supplier.
* Scrapscreens are easily damaged. This one shows clearly the warping and crinkling that can occur. Obviously, the less damaged examples are more valuable.

Decalcomania
Decalcomania, a type of glass wares decorated by amateurs with a variety of scraps and pictures, has become very collectable recently. The scraps were glued to the inside of a clear glass vessel, and were then coated with whitewash or enamel. The vase shown *above* (together with a detail of the inside of the lid) is typical.

Next to vases (also sometimes referred to as *pot-au-cheminée* or fireplace vases), the most sought-after examples of decalcomania are those items enigmatically referred to as "witches' balls" – globes of glass decorated through a tiny hole with scraps and then sealed by pouring white paint into the hole. (Technically, "witches' balls" were of mirrored glass, and were hung in cottage windows to ward off witches, who were said to fear their own reflection.)
* Condition is crucial. Whitewash tends to flake and erode, seriously reducing value.

Scraps were also pasted into albums, like the example *above*. As with screens, the more unusual and attractive the arrangement of the scraps, the more desirable the piece is overall, especially if the scraps are pasted on one side of the page only.

OTHER COLLECTABLES

Kitchen wares

This surprisingly fruitful collecting area includes various time-saving devices such as marmalade cutters and sugar nips, and other kitchen items, such as jelly moulds and peeling devices.

Fans

Fans were used as accessories on special occasions. The French used chromolithography to emulate the extravagant 18thC hand-painted fans; ivory and mother-of-pearl fans continued to be imported from China. Fans were also used to advertise wares or as souvenirs: this American wood and paper example commemorates a hundred years of the International Exhibition at the Independence Hall in Philadelphia.

The Victorian age saw the invention of many irons with specific functions relevant to fashions of the day. For example, fluters, crimpers and goffering irons were designed to put pleats into fabrics. This is a good example of a double goffering iron – the projecting poker pulls out, is heated and then replaced. Starched material is pressed against the other end and is crimped. Good examples like this one, with its black japanned base and gilt highlighting, are keenly sought by collectors today, as are more conventional flatirons.

Tunbridge ware

This stationery box is in Tunbridge ware: a mosaic created by gluing together slender rods of wood of different colours and grain within a framework. The pieces were sliced crossways to obtain as many pictures as there were slices.

Pictures

This Napier Patent Coffee Making Machine of 1845 is one of many mid-19thC coffee machines patented in response to the growing vogue for coffee. Examples retaining their original copper and glass burner and beaker, as this one does, command a premium.

Pictures were made from a variety of media during the Victorian period, including cork and seaweed. Cork pictures were made in Britain and on the Continent, and many of those found today were made in China for export. Subjects include windmills, German and Dutch scenes, and English views and buildings: the boxed and glazed cork picture *above* shows a naive view of Windsor Castle.

AMERICAN FOLK ART

Folk art is a broad term for the great variety of naively executed objects produced in the United States by untrained people to decorate their homes or places of work. The most common areas of interest for collectors include:
* "naive" or "primitive" paintings (usually small) dating from the 18th and 19thC depicting domestic scenes, landscapes or portraits (particularly of children) that tend to be composed and drawn in a childlike manner
* folk sculpture and decorative wood carvings of all descriptions
* weathervanes and other metalwork
* scrimshaw (carved shell or bone)
* all kinds of homemade furniture and furnishings, including textiles, lighting, furniture, toys and agricultural and domestic utensils.

The most collectable pieces of folk art display typically American motifs, such as the American flag, eagles, and Indians. The carved wooden eagle, *above*, is in painted pine and carries a seasonal message. Particularly large numbers of these eagles were produced around the time of the American Centennial celebrations of 1876. Painted flags were also typical.
* Strangely, objects produced by American Indians are not considered true folk art, although they are keenly collected.
* Objects produced by puritanical sects are especially collectable, and there is a sub-category of small, wooden objects such as boxes and picture frames made by hobos, and known as "tramp art".

Wood carvings
This is a particularly wide collecting area, comprising pieces that vary in scale from whirligigs (mechanical, wind-driven ornaments), to carousel figures, such as this figure of a black man *right*, made in New York in the late 19thC of carved and painted pine. It is almost lifesize – cigar store Indians, such as this, were designed to stand outside stores as an advertisement – and are sometimes larger than lifesize. Most tend to be vibrantly polychromatic.
* These sculptures were exposed to wind and rain, and many have been repainted or repaired. Items in their original state are highly sought-after, even if in poor condition.

Weathervanes

American weathervanes were often made commercially, but today they are widely collected because of their association with the country's early settlers and their frequently innovative designs. The vane illustrated *above*, is based on the popular "Running Horse" design. Most examples are constructed from two pieces of sheet copper welded into a pocket to hold an armature. Simple, home-made weathervanes were usually cut from a single sheet of thin metal and then fixed to a post. Some retain their original decoration or gilding, although many of them are undecorated or lack their original polychrome.

* Weathervanes are particularly susceptible to being faked and, as reproductions are difficult to spot, the available provenance of a piece adds considerably to the value.

Scrimshaw

Most American scrimshaw takes the form of maritime images engraved onto whalebone or narwhal tusks, either by mariners or others working in the American whaling industry based in the northeast of the United States. Many examples are signed and dated, and the earliest known pieces were made in the late 17thC. The highest prices are fetched by excellent examples of characteristic carvings, or those with an interesting provenance or unusual design.

This fine carved whalebone jagging wheel (used to make patterns on the edges of pastry crusts) was made in New England, c.1870. Many small household utensils for sewing, baking and whaling were fashioned in scrimshaw, and most pieces found today date from the peak years of the whaling industry, c.1825-75.

Collecting

Most pieces available today were made in the late 19th and early 20thC. However, with folk art, age does not necessarily equal value; the crucial factors are the degree of naiveté and of freedom from convention and commercialism.

The relative simplicity of most American folk art makes it a popular area for imitation. Be particularly wary of synthetic bone scrimshaw (which is abundant, convincing and expensive) and sheet copper weathervanes with a modern verdigris patina.

GLOSSARY

Acid cutting A method of decorating glass by which the objects are coated with an acid-resistant substance such as wax, then incised with a fine steel point and dipped in acid.

Aesthetic Movement An artistic movement prevalent in Britain c.1860–c.1880, which advocated a return to a harmony of form and function in design and decoration.

Ambrotype A type of photograph achieved by exposing a glass plate treated with the wet collodion chemical process. The resulting negative image was made positive by backing with black paper or paint.

Appliqué The decorative application of a second fabric to the main fabric ground.

Arts & Crafts A late-19thC artistic movement led by William Morris (see pp.24-5 and pp.154-5) which advocated a return to medieval standards of craftsmanship and simplicity of design.

Automata A term covering a variety of mechanical toys, usually clockwork, popular during the 18th and 19thC.

Biscuit The term for unglazed porcelain fired only once.

Bisque A type of doll whose name derives from "biscuit", being made of unglazed china.

Britannia metal A popular 19thC pewter substitute, an alloy of tin, antimony and a trace of copper.

Burmese ware A type of art glass made by combining gold and uranium oxides.

Cameo glass Decorative wares composed of two or more layers of glass laminated together, often of varying colours, carved on a wheel or etched to make a design in relief.

Cased glass (overlay) Similar to cameo glass, but with the design on the outer layer cut away rather than in relief.

Case furniture Furniture intended primarily as a receptacle, such as chests of drawers.

Chasing A method of embossing or engraving metal, particularly silver.

Chatelaine An ornamental device or belt worn at the waist, with a series of hooks, to hold household keys, watch, scissors and so on.

Cire perdue ("lost wax") The French term for a process of casting sculpture that results in unique casts.

Composition A tough combination of wood pulp and paper, used in the making of dolls.

Copper electrotyping A more refined version of the **electroplating** process.

Crazing The break-up of a glazed surface into a fine network of cracks, either intentionally or as a result of age.

Daguerreotype An early form of photograph, and the first to be made generally available.

Davenport A small decorative writing desk with a sloped top and drawers below.

Decalcomania Victorian glass wares decorated by amateurs with a variety of scraps and pictures.

Earthenware The term for any pottery that has not been vitrified (ie. treated to achieve a glassy surface). Hence, all pottery except stoneware.

Ebonized wood Wood stained to resemble ebony.

Electroplating The process whereby silver is electronically deposited on a copper, nickel silver or Britannia metal base.

Epergne A type of ornamental glass flower stand, produced mainly in Stourbridge.

Flatback A term for Staffordshire portrait figures with flat, undecorated backs, designed to stand against a wall or on a mantelpiece.

Flatware The technical term for any flat or shallow tableware, such as plates, more specifically applied to cutlery.

Glaze The smooth, shiny coating to **soft-paste porcelain** or **stoneware**

Hallmark The marks stamped on silver or gold pieces when passed at assay (the test for quality). Books are available that list all the relevant date, place and maker's marks. However, while hallmarks are a good guide to age and authenticity, they should not be regarded as definitive, as they can be worn, faked, or even let in from another piece.

Hard-paste porcelain The term for porcelain made using the ancient Chinese combination of kaolin and petuntse.

Imari A type of Japanese porcelain with heavy decoration inspired by brocade designs painted in iron red and cobalt blue.

Impressed Indented, as opposed to incised.

Incised Decoration or maker's

mark cut or scratched into the surface, rather than impressed.

Indigo A blue vegetable-based dye used in the colouring of textiles.

Ironstone china Hard white earthenware made to imitate the earthenware patented by Masons (see pp. 60-61) in 1813.

Iznik A type of boldly coloured Turkish pottery.

Jardinière A plant container made from a variety of materials including glass or pottery.

Latticinio A type of decoration on glasswares which consists of thin white canes of opaque glass moulded on to a piece to create a latticework or lace effect.

Lustreware Pottery with a polished surface produced using metallic pigments, usually siver or copper.

Madder The red vegetable-based dye used in the colouring of textiles.

Majolica Painted, brightly-coloured earthenware produced in large quantities in Britain and Europe from c.1850.

Nailsea glass A type of wares produced at the Nailsea works and elsewhere in England, decorated by the fusing or splashing on to the glass body of pieces of coloured or white enamel.

Novelty or "fancy" glass The elaborately coloured and novel glass produced by several factories from the mid-19thC.

Opaline glass The semi-opaque white (opalescent) glass produced in 19thC France.

Parian A type of porcelain made with a matt, semi-translucent, ivory-coloured body which resembles marble and was developed as a substitute for the white biscuit figures popularized by Sèvres and others in the 18th and early 19thC.

Pâte-sur-pâte A form of ceramic decoration whereby white slip is applied and fired in layer upon layer until the build-up creates a cameo effect.

Patina The fine layer or surface sheen on metal or furniture that results with time, use or chemical corrosion.

Peachblow The American term for shaded glass similar to **Burmese ware**, with an inner layer of opalescent glass giving the appearance of glazed porcelain.

Pontil mark The mark left by the iron rod upon which some glass is supported for final shaping after blowing.

Pressed glass, or slagware Glass items produced in a mechanical press mould.

Quercitron A yellow vegetable-based dye used in the colouring of textiles.

Repoussé A term for metalwork decoration beaten in relief from the reverse side.

Reticulated The term used of the thinly-walled porcelain pieces with intricate pierced decoration produced by Worcester Royal Porcelain in the late 19thC.

Rock crystal A form of engraved lead glass cut and polished to simulate the natural facets of actual rock crystal.

Sand-cast A method of casting bronze in a mould made from pounded quartz and sand.

Scrimshaw The term for carved items made from shell or bone, usually by mariners, popular in the United States in the 19thC.

Sgraffito A form of earthenware decoration incised through **slip**, revealing the contrasting ground beneath.

Shades Peculiarly Victorian table decorations of imitation flowers, stuffed birds or miniature figures covered by a glass dome.

"Silvered" glass The term for items produced by injecting silver between two layers of glass.

Slip A smooth dilution of clay and water used in the making and decoration of pottery.

Soft-paste porcelain The term for porcelain made using a combination of kaolin and powdered glass, soapstone or calcined bone.

Stilt mark The mark left on the base of some pottery by supports used during firing.

Stoneware Non-porous pottery, a hybrid of earthenware and porcelain, made of clay and a fusible substance.

Underglaze The coloured decorative layer applied under the main glaze.

Vaseline A type of ornamental, semi-translucent yellow glass popular in Britain, Europe and the United States in the late 19thC.

Vitro porcelain British art glass made from slag, cryolite and glass metal, giving a streaked opaque green effect, with purple veining.

Verdigris The green or bluish **patina** formed on copper, brass, or bronze.

Weld A yellow vegetable-based dye used in the colouring of textiles.

Whitework The name for a type of fine embroidery in white thread on muslin or fine cotton pioneered in Ayrshire c.1814. Also known as "Ayrshire" embroidery.

SELECTED DESIGNERS, MANUFACTURERS & RETAILERS

Page references in brackets refer to fuller entries given elsewhere.

Alcock, Samuel (dates unknown)
English potter; his factory at Corbridge operated 1830-1859.

Ashbee, Charles Robert (1863-1942)
English architect and designer associated with the Arts and Crafts movement. In 1888, founded the Guild of Handicraft in order to perpetuate the ideals of medieval craft guilds. Ashbee and Guild marks are stamped. (pp.132-3)

Baccarat (established 1764)
Alsatian glassworks famous for its paperweights. Marks: stamped or etched. (pp.44-5)

Bailey, E. H. (1788-1867)
English artist and sculptor in the Neo-classical style. (p.99)

Barye, Antoine-Louis (1796-1875)
French animalier. Favoured the *cire perdue* method of casting, resulting in unique casts.(p.101)

Belleek (established 1863)
Irish ceramics firm. Specialized in openwork baskets. Wares often impressed on the underside with "Belleek". From 1863 to c.1880, Belleek wares also carried a printed black mark of a seated Irish wolfhound, harp and round tower. After 1880, "County Fermanagh" was added. (p.57)

Belter, John Henry (1804-63)
German-born cabinet-maker active in the United States. Gave his name to a style of large-scale, elaborate Rococo furniture. (pp.30-1)

Benson, William Arthur Smith (1854-1924)
English architect, furniture and metalwork designer.Best known for his light fittings and tableware. Close friend of **William Morris**, of whose Merton Abbey workshop he became Managing Director in 1896. Marks: stamped. (pp. 136-7)

Berlin (established 1751)
German porcelain factory. Marks: in mid-19thC, painted red orb or underglaze blue painted sceptre; plaques also carry initials KPM.

Bevan, Charles (active 1860s)
English designer and manufacturer of furniture, specializing in Gothic-revival style.

Bonheur, Rosa (1822-99) and Isidore (1827-1901)
French brother and sister animaliers. (p.103)

Boston and Sandwich Glass Company (established 1826)
American glass manufacturers, formerly the Sandwich Manufacturing Company. Made pressed glass novelties and a huge variety of glass paperweights. Later incorporated into **New England Glass Company** (p. 51).

Brannam, Charles (1855-1937)
English art potter. Pieces are often signed and dated.

Brownfield, William (active 1850-91)
English potter and porcelain manufacturer in Staffordshire. Produced high quality earthenware and porcelain, largely for export. Marks: double globe with BROWNFIELD & SON, COBRIDGE STAFFS on ribbon, or either WB or BROWNFIELD impressed.

Bru (Bru Jeune & Cie) (established 1866)
French doll manufacturers famous for their bisque dolls. (p.162)

Burges, William (1827-81)
English architect and furniture designer in the early Gothic style. (pp. 18-9)

Butler, Frank A. (late 19th–early 20thC)
English pottery decorator. Worked for **Doulton** in a distinctive style sometimes involving bosses formed by relief modelling.

Century Guild, The
English Arts and Crafts society of designers, artists, architects and metalworkers, founded c.1882 by **Arthur Mackmurdo** to restore responsibility for the decorative crafts to the artist from the tradesman. Marks: on metalwork – hammered mark; on textiles – printed initials. (pp.26-7)

Clichy (established 1837)
French glassworks at Billancourt, Paris, best known for their paperweights. Merged with Sèvres glassworks in 1875. (p.51)

Coalbrookdale (active 19thC)
English iron foundry near Ironbridge, Shropshire. Largest 19thC manufacturer of iron furniture. Some designs by **Christopher Dresser**. (pp. 134-5)

Coalport (established 1796)
English ceramics firm. Produced Sèvres-style wares, some bearing paintings of exotic birds. Some wares are marked Coalport AD 1750. (p.56)

Collinson & Lock (estab. 1870, absorbed into Gillow, 1897)
London furniture makers in the Aesthetic style. Designers included **Talbert, Godwin** and **Collcutt**.

Collcutt, Thomas Edward (1840-1924)
English furniture designer. Worked primarily for **Collinson and Lock**, specializing in ebonized furniture.

J.G. Crace & Sons (1745-1899)
London-based furniture makers known for their Gothic-revival pieces designed by, among others, **Godwin, Pugin** and **Voysey** (pp.16-7 and pp.22-3).

Crane, Walter (1845-1915)
English painter, graphic artist and designer associated with the Arts and Crafts movement. Designed pottery and tiles for **Wedgwood, Minton,** Pilkington and **Maw & Co.** Mark: painted monogram. Designed textiles for **Morris and Co.**

Crossley (active 19thC)
English textile and carpet manufacturer at Halifax, Yorkshire. Pioneered mechanization in weaving.

Dearle, John Henry (1890-1932)
English porcelain decorator. Pieces usually signed.

de Morgan, William (1839-1917)
English ceramic designer connected with the Arts and Crafts Movement. Founded the William de Morgan Pottery (in 1872) and other works. Marks: impressed. (pp.74-5)

Derby (c.1749-present)
Renowned English porcelain factory. Variety of marks incorporating the word Derby.

Doulton (1815-present)
English ceramics factory at Lambeth, best known for salt-glaze stoneware. (pp.76-6)

Dresser, Christopher (1834-1904)
Scottish-born botanist, designer and writer. Most famous for silver and metalwork designs for various firms, including **Elkington, Coalbrookdale** and Benham & Froud. Marks: on glass – etched; on metalwork – stamped. (pp. 130-1)

Eastlake, Charles Locke (1836-1906)
English architect and furniture designer of the Gothic revival. (pp.20-1)

Elkington & Co. (c.1830-present)
English silversmith founded by George Elkington, who, with his cousin Henry, patented their electroplating process in 1840. Marks: stamped. (pp.126-7)

Elton, Sir Edmund (1846-1920)
English baronet and self-taught potter. Produced art pottery on his Somerset estate, first as the Sunflower Pottery but later under the name Elton Ware. Mark: painted. (pp.86-7)

Fox (active mid 19thC)
London-based family firm of silversmiths. Charles Fox Junior took over from his father c.1822; joined by sons Charles (C.T.) and George c.1841.

Fratin, Christophe (1800-64)
German-born sculptor and animalier who worked in France. Famous for anthropomorphic pieces. (pp.102-3)

Fremiet Emanuel (1824-1910)
French sculptor and animalier, who made popular, sentimental representations. (pp.102-3)

Gallé, Émile (1846-1904)
Foremost French glassmaker, ceramist and designer. Marks: on glass – large variety of etched marks; on furniture – signature in marquetry. (pp.46-7)

R. & S. Garrard (c.1819-present)
London retailer and jeweller, appointed Crown Jewellers in 1843. 19thC wares are marked "RG". (pp.128-9)

Gillow (estab'd 1695, active today as Waring and Gillow)
Established in Lancaster by Robert Gillow. Specialized in reproducing fine quality antique furniture.

Gibson, John (1790-1866)
English sculptor working strictly in the Neo-classical style. (p.98)

Gilbert, Sir Alfred (1854-1934)
English sculptor and exponent of the New Sculpture. (pp.106-7)

Godwin, Edward William (1833-86)
English designer in the Aesthetic style. (pp.22-3, 152-3)

Gorham Corporation, The (established 1813)
Important American silversmiths and jewellers. Produced mainly decorative tablewares in the Rococo style. Marks: stamped. (pp.138-9)

Martelé
950-1000 FINE

Grainger, G & Co (established 1801, absorbed into Worcester Royal Porcelain Co. 1899)
Founded in Worcester, Grainger initially followed the Rococo style. Later diversified into domestic and reticulated wares, often with *pâte-sur-pâte* decoration. Mark (1889-1902 – ROYAL CHINA WORKS WORCESTER surrounding G&Co ESTABLISHED 1801.

Grueby, William H. (1867-1925)
American potter. Founded Grueby Faience Company at Boston, Massachusetts in 1894. Produced tiles, vases and art pottery.

Hadley, James (1837-1903)
English ceramic modeller and designer. Worked at **Worcester.** Notable for pieces in the Kate Greenaway and Japanese style. Later sold own porcelain as Hadley ware, a business continued by his sons until sold to Worcester in 1905. (p.67)

Herter Brothers (established 1865)
American furniture makers founded in New York by the half-brothers Gustave and Christian Herter. The latter's pieces, inspired by the English Aesthetic movement, are the most important. (pp.32-3)

Hobbs, Brockunier (established 1845)
American glass company founded in Virginia. Famous for Peachblow wares.

Holland & Sons (established early 18thC)
London-based funiture makers of high-quality pieces for royal residences. Pieces reflect the 18thC designs of Adam and Chippendale.

Howell & James (active 19thC)
London pottery retailers who sold undecorated wares which were then painted by amateurs and offered for sale. Base wares often came from reputable factories and can be misleadingly stamped to infer factory decoration.

Hunt & Roskill (estab. 1843)
Formerly **Storr** & Mortimer. Important silversmiths headed by Storr's nephew, the silversmith, John Samuel Hunt. (p. 129)

Hurten, Charles Ferdinand (1813-1901)
German-born ceramic decorator. Worked in France and England, for Sèvres and Copeland among others. Produced mainly realistic paintings of flora and fauna.

Image, Selwyn (1849-1930)
English illustrator and designer. Designed panels and inlay decoration, often for Mackmurdo

and the **Century Guild**. Marks: printed initials.

SJ

Jackson and Graham (estab'd 1840, absorbed by Collinson & Lock, 1885)
English cabinet-makers renowned for their excessively ornate pieces.
Jackson & Sons (active 19thC)
English furniture makers who specialized in *papier mâché* furniture.
Jennens & Bettridge (active 1816–64)
British furniture makers, best known for their *papier mâché* furniture. (pp.14-5)
Jones, George (died 1893)
English potter. Worked at the **Minton** factory before founding the Trent Pottery. (pp.68-9)
Jones, Owen (1809-74)
English architect, designer and illustrator. Superintendent of Works at the Great Exhibition of 1851. (p.144)
Jumeau (1842-99)
French doll manufacturers, specialized in bisque and fashion dolls. (p.162)

DÉPOSÉ
E. 7 J.

Kerr & Binns (1852-62)
From 1852, the name for the partnership that in 1862 became the Royal Worcester Porcelain Company. Made mainly table wares in porcelain. (p.66)
Knowles, Taylor and Knowles (established 1854)
American pottery at East Liverpool, Ohio. Produced cream coloured earthenware and semi-porcelain. Marks: star-shaped motif or bison and KT&K in a rectangle or circle.
Leighton, Frederick Lord (1830-96)
English painter, sculptor and pioneer of the "New Sculpture". (pp.104-5)
Liberty & Co. (1875-present)
English retailer famous for textiles and metalwork. Their "Art Fabrics" incorporated Art Nouveau elements into Aesthetic designs. Marks: on metalwork – stamped. (pp.130-1 and 156-7)

Lonhuda (established 1892)
American art pottery. From c.1890 produced pieces resembling the successful **Rookwood** wares. Marks: impressed.

McCallum & Hodson (19thC)
English manufacturers of *papier mâché* furniture.
Mackennal, Sir Edgar Bertram (1863-1931)
Australian sculptor inspired by French Symbolism and Romanticism. (pp.108-9)
Mackmurdo, Arthur Heygate (1851-1942)
English architect and founder of the **Century Guild**. Marks: hammered initial. (pp.26-7)

M

Marshall, Mark V. (died 1912)
English designer, **Doulton** potter and sculptor, best known for grotesque animal jugs.
Mason, C. J. (1813-62)
English potter and founder of Masons. Patented ironstone in 1813, and became the foremost maker. (pp.60-1)
Maw and Co. (active second half 19thC)
Largest English tile manufacturer of the 19thC, based in Shropshire. Produced tiles using a number of processes and styles, including majolica, mosaic and moulded relief. Later expanded into general ceramic production.
Mêne, Pierre Jule (1810-79)
Prominent and prolific French animalier. (p.100)
Minton & Co. (British, 1793-present, from 1873, Mintons)
Staffordshire pottery. Produced high-quality earthenware and porcelain, but best known for its majolica wares and art pottery. Marks: printed. (pp.70-3)

Moigniez, Jules (1835-94)
French animalier best known for his bird sculptures. (p.102)
Morris, William (1834-96)
English poet, writer, socialist and

designer. Founded Marshall,
Faulkner & Co in 1861 (became
Morris & Co.) to execute his
designs for furniture, textiles and
wallpapers. (pp.24-5, 154-5)

**Mount Washington Glass
Company (established 1837)**
American glassworks established
near Boston by William L.
Libbey. Produced art glass and
was closely associated with the
American Aesthetic Movement.
(pp.50-1)
**Nekola, Karel (active from
c.1880)**
Bohemian artist and potter. From
1883 worked at the Fife Pottery
decorating **Wemyss** ware, with
which his name, and that of his
son, Joseph (died 1952) are now
synonymous. (pp.90-1)
**New England Glass Company
(1818-88)**
American glass company.
Produced coloured art glass and
paperweights. (pp.50-1)
Owens, J.B. (died 1934)
American potter and founder of
the Roseville factory in Ohio
(1890). Made majolica wares and
copies of the successful wares of
Rookwood. Marks: Roseville –
impressed; J.B. Owens – printed.
(pp.95)

**Phoenixville Pottery (c.1867-
1902)**
American pottery, the largest and
most influential manufacturer of
American majolica. (p.92-3)
**Pinder, Bourne & Co. (estab'd
1862, taken over by Doulton &
Co. in 1882)**
Pottery manufacturers in Burslem,
Staffordshire producing mainly
tablewares. Japanese-inspired
design is typical. Mark: PINDER
BOURNE & Co/NILE St/
BURSLEM.

Powell, James (1835-1914)
English maker of Art glass.
Designs are generally lighter than
most Victorian cut glass. His
designers included Phillip Webb
and Joseph Leicester. Marks:
stamped. (pp.48-9)
Pratt, F. & R. (active 19thC)
Staffordshire pottery which
perfected the technique of multi-
coloured printing on a white
earthenware base, now often
referred to as Prattware. Some
pieces are marked "F & R
PRATT FENTON", impressed.
(p.61)
**Pugin, Augustus Welby
Northmore (1812-52)**
English furniture designer whose
work epitomizes the Gothic
revival in Britain. Produced solid
and utilitarian furniture, usually of
oak. (pp.16-7, 144-5)
**Ridgway, Edward John (active
early 19thC-c.1872)**
Staffordshire potter best known
for tea and dessert services in
bone china, earthenware and
stoneware. Mark: Staffordshire
knot. (pp.60-1)
**Robinson & Leadbeater (1856-
1924)**
Staffordshire pottery renowned
for its Parian ware. Victorian
pieces are marked with an "RL"
surrounded by an oval border.
Rockingham (c.1826-42)
English porcelain factory at
Swinton, Yorkshire. Mark: a
griffen; red on wares made before
1830, puce thereafter.
Rookwood (1880-1941)
American pottery founded in
Cincinnatti by Maria Longworth
Nichols. Best-known of the
American producers of art pottery,
particularly in the Japanese style.
Marks: raised. (pp.94-5)

**Rundell, Bridge & Rundell
(1805-39)**
London gold and silversmiths.
Crown Jewellers before Garrard.
Designers included John Flaxman
and Philip Storr.

Saunders, Gaulbert (active mid-19thC)
Furniture designer in the Gothic style.

Silver Studio (1880-1965)
London design studio opened by Arthur Silver (1853-96). Known for wallpapers and textiles. (p.157)

Sowerby (1847-1972)
English glassworks in Gateshead on Tyne famous for pressed glass and vitro-porcelain in the Aesthetic style. Mark: a peacock's head.

Stevens & Williams (c.1880-present)
Stourbridge factory, renowned for novelty glass. Later Brierley Royal Crystal. Mark: etched or impressed "Stevens & Williams" or "S&W".

Paul Storr (active early 19thC)
Most famous 19thC English silversmith. Best known for Neo-classical pieces in silver-gilt. In 1822 founded. (pp. 128-9).

Stourbridge
English glass-making centre in the Midlands known for cameo glass by Thomas Webb & Sons and novelty, or "fancy", glass produced by several factories. (pp.36-9)

Talbert, Bruce (1838-81)
Scottish-born architect and furniture designer. Designs tend to be massive and profusely inlaid, showing elements of both the Neo-gothic and the Aesthetic styles. (pp. 20-1, 152-3)

Taylor, Smith & Taylor (established 1896)
American pottery at East Liverpool, Ohio. Produced earthenware and ironstone china. Marks: impressed.

Templeton, James (born 1802)
Scottish textile and carpet manufacturer. Founded factory in Glasgow in 1839, which still produces carpets on the biggest looms in Britain. (p. 148)

Thornycroft, Sir William Hamo (1850-1925)
English sculptor and exponent of the New Sculpture, who drew his subjects mainly from Greek mythology. (pp. 110-1)

Tiffany & Co. (1837-present)
American jeweller and retailer founded by Charles Louis Tiffany (1812-1902) and John B. Mill Young. Now established in Geneva, Paris, New York and London. Marks: stamped. (pp.122-3)

Voysey, Charles Annesley (1847-1941)
English architect. Designed interiors, wallpapers, textiles and furniture. (pp.28-9, 156)

William Watt & Co.(active 1865-85)
London-based furniture makers known for pieces in the Anglo-Japanese style.

Thomas Webb & Sons (1856-present)
Stourbridge firm renowned for cameo glass, Burmese ware and rock crystal. Marks: printed or etched. (pp.38-9)

Wedgwood, Josiah, & Sons (1759-present)
Renowned English pottery founded in Staffordshire by Josiah Wedgwood. Produced an extensive range of decorative and useful wares. 19thC pieces included porcelain, parian ware, stone china, creamware, majolica and jasper ware.

Worcester Royal Porcelain Company (active 1783-1902)
English porcelain factory. Became the Worcester Royal Porcelain Company in 1862, producing a wide variety of excellent porcelain wares. Important designers of the Victorian period included **James Hadley** and Thomas Bott. (pp.66-7)

REGISTRATION AND DESIGN MARKS

Design registration

The protection of designs by official registration was first practiced in 1842. The mark was a diamond shape which included numbers indicating the date of registration and the batch number. Each category of wares was indicated by a roman numeral – III for glass, IV for ceramics. In 1868 the positioning of the date letters within the diamond was changed.

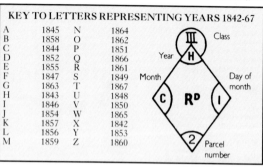

KEY TO LETTERS REPRESENTING YEARS 1842-67

A	1845	N	1864	
B	1858	O	1862	
C	1844	P	1851	
D	1852	Q	1866	
E	1855	R	1861	
F	1847	S	1849	
G	1863	T	1867	
H	1843	U	1848	
I	1846	V	1850	
J	1854	W	1865	
K	1857	X	1842	
L	1856	Y	1853	
M	1859	Z	1860	

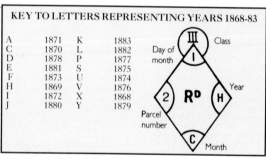

KEY TO LETTERS REPRESENTING YEARS 1868-83

A	1871	K	1883
C	1870	L	1882
D	1878	P	1877
E	1881	S	1875
F	1873	U	1874
H	1869	V	1876
I	1872	X	1868
J	1880	Y	1879

KEY TO LETTERS USED FOR MONTHS

A	December	E	May	K	November		
B	October	G	February	M	June		
C	January	H	April	R	August		
D	September	I	July	W	March		

In 1883 the diamond was abandoned and all categories of furnishings and decorative and applied arts were now marked with a series of numbers sometimes accompanied by the words Reg or Rd No.

REGISTRATION NUMBERS 1884-1901

1884	1	1890	141273	1896	268392
1885	19754	1891	163767	1897	291241
1886	40480	1892	185713	1898	311658
1887	64520	1893	205240	1899	331707
1888	90483	1894	224720	1900	351202
1889	116648	1895	246975	1901	368154

BIBLIOGRAPHY

GENERAL

Anscombe and Gere, *Arts and Crafts in Britain and America*, London, 1978

Aslin, Elizabeth, *The Aesthetic Movement*, London, 1969

Field, Rachel, *Victoriana*, London, 1988

Fine Art Society, The, *The Architect-Designers Pugin to Mackintosh*, London, 1981

Ffrench, Y., *The Great Exhibition*, London, 1950

Gibbs-Smith, C.H., *The Great Exhibition of 1851: A Commemorative Album*, London, 1950

Gilbert, Alfred, *Royal Academy of Arts 1986*, Exhibition Catalogue

Haslam, Malcolm, *Arts and Crafts*, London, 1988

Marks and Monograms of the Modern Movement 1815-1930, London, 1977

Henderson, Philip, *William Morris*, London, 1967

Home, Bea, *Antiques from the Victorian Home*, London, 1973

Kaplan, Wendy, (Ed.) *Encyclopedia of Arts and Crafts The International Arts Movement 1850-1920*, London, 1989

Laver, J., *Victoriana*, London, 1972

May, John, *Victoria Remembered*, London, 1983

Metropolitan Museum of Art, *In Pursuit of Beauty*, New York, 1986

Naylor, Gillian, *The Arts and Crafts Movement*, London, 1971

Pevsner, Nikolaus, *High Victorian Design: a study of the exhibits of 1851*, 1951

Priestly, J.B., *Victoria's Heyday*, London, 1972

Strong, Roy, *The Collector's Encyclopedia Victoriana to Art Deco*, London, 1974

Ward Lock, *Dictionary of Turn of the Century Antiques*, London, 1974

Watkinson, Ray, *William Morris as a Designer*, London, 1967

Watkinson, Raymond, *Pre-Raphaelite Art and Design*, London, 1970

FURNITURE

Aguis, Pauline, *British Furniture 1880-1915*, Woodbridge, 1978

Aslin, Elizabeth, *The Furniture Designs of E.W. Godwin*, London, 1970

Nineteenth Century English Furniture, London, 1962

Jervis, Simon, *Victorian Furniture*, London, 1968

Stanton, Phoebe, *Pugin*, London, 1971

Symonds, Robert and Bruce Whineray, *Victorian Furniture*, London, 1962

GLASS

Beard, Geoffrey W., *Nineteenth Century Cameo Glass*, Monmouthshire, 1956

Davis, Derek, *English Bottles and Decanters 1650-1900*, London, 1972

Dodsworth, Roger, *Glass and Glassmakers*, Risborough, 1982

Gardner, P.V., *The Glass of Frederick Carder*, New York, 1971

George, S. and Helen McKearin, *American Glass*, New York, 1968

Grover, Ray and Lee, *Art Glass Nouveau*, Vermont, 1967

Haynes, E. Barrington, *Glass Through the Ages*, London, 1948

Lee, Ruth Webb, *Nineteenth Century Art Glass*, New York, 1952

Mackay, James, *Glass Paperweights*, London, 1973

O'Looney, Betty, *Victorian Glass*, London, 1972

Revi, Albert C., *American Art Nouveau Glass*, New Jersey, 1968

American Pressed Glass and Figure Bottles, New York, 1964

Nineteenth Century Glass. Its Genesis and Development, New York, 1959

Slack, R., *English Pressed Glass 1830-1900*, London, 1987

Wakefield, Hugh, *Nineteenth Century British Glass*, London, 1961

Wotley, Raymond, *Pressed Flint-Glass*, Risborough, 1986

Carnival Glass, Risborough, 1983

CERAMICS

Atterbury, P., *Dictionary of Minton*, Woodbridge, 1989

Austwick, J. and B., *The Decorated Tile*, London, 1980

Barnard, Julian, *Victorian Ceramic Tiles*, London, 1972

Batkin, Maureen, *Wedgwood Ceramics 1846-1959*, London, 1982

Bergesen, V., *Majolica British Continental and American Wares*, London, 1989

Berthoud, M., *Daniel – Porcelain*, Bridgenorth, 1980

Cecil, V., *Minton Majolica*, London, 1982

Charleston, R.J., *World Ceramics*, Feltham, 1968

Cox, and Cox, *Rockingham Pottery and Porcelain*, London, 1983

Dawes, Nicholas M., *Majolica*, New York, 1990

Dennis, Richard, *Doulton Stoneware and Terracotta 1870-1925* London, 1971

185

Doulton Pottery Stoneware Terracotta 1870-1928 London, 1971

Doulton Pottery Lambeth to Burslem 1873-1939, London, 1975

The Parian Phenomenon, London, 1989

Royal Doulton 1815-1965, London, 1965

Gaunt, W. and M.D.E. Clayton-Stamm, *William de Morgan*, London, 1971

Gilbert, Alfred *English Art Pottery 1865-1915*, Woodbridge, 1975

Godden, G.A., *An Illustrated Encyclopaedia of British Pottery and Porcelain*, London, 1968

Coalport and Coalbrookdale Porcelain, London, 1970

Encyclopaedia of British Pottery and Porcelain Marks, London, 1964

The Illustrated Guide to Mason's Ironstone China, London, 1971

Ridgway Porcelains, London, 1972

Staffordshire Porcelain, St Albans, 1983

Victorian Porcelain, London, 1961

Haggar, R.G., *Staffordshire Chimney Ornaments*, London, 1955

Hall, John, *Staffordshire Portrait Figures*, London, 1972

Haslam, Malcolm, *English Art Pottery 1865-1915*, Woodbridge, 1975

The Martin Brothers Potters, London, 1978

Hawes, Lloyd E., *The Dedham Pottery*, Massachusetts, 1969

Henzke, Lucile, *American Art Pottery*, New Jersey, 1970

Hughes, G.B., *Victorian Pottery and Porcelain*, London, 1959

Le Vine, J.R.A., *Linthorpe Pottery, Yorkshire*, 1970

Locket, T.A., *Victorian Tiles*, Woodbridge

Luysen, Alice Cooney Freling, *American Porcelain 1770-1920*, New York, 1989

Mankowitze, Wolf, *Wedgwood*, London, 1953

Oliver, Anthony, *Staffordshire Pottery – The Tribal Art of England*, London, 1981

The Victorian Staffordshire Figure, London, 1971

Peck, Herbert, *The Book of Rookwood Pottery*, New York, 1968

Pugh, P.D. Gordon, *Staffordshire Portrait Figures*, London, 1970

Rogers De Rin Collection, The, *Wemyss Ware 1880-1915*, Exhibition at Sotheby's, London, 1976

Sandon, H. and J., *Graingers Worcester Porcelain*, London, 1989

Scudan, Henry, *Royal Worcester Porcelain*, London, 1973

Shinn, Charles and Dorie, *The Illustrated Guide to Victorian Parian China*, London, 1971

Thomas, E. Lloyd, *Victorian Art Pottery*, London, 1974

Twitchett, J. and B. Bailey, *Royal Crown Derby Porcelain*, Woodbridge, 1988

Victoria and Albert Museum, *Catalogue of works by William de Morgan*, London, 1921

Wakefield, Hugh, *Victorian Pottery*, London, 1962

Williams-Wood, Cyril, *Staffordshire Pot Lids and their Potters*, London, 1972

SCULPTURE

Beattie, Susan, *The New Sculpture*, London, 1983

Cooper, Jeremy, *Nineteenth Century Romantic Bronzes*, Devon, 1974

Handley-Read, Charles, *British Sculpture, 1850-1914*, London, 1968

Horsewell, Jane, *Bronze Sculptures of 'Les Animaliers'*, Suffolk, 1971

Mackay, J., *The Animaliers*, London, 1973

Saulnier, C. *Antoine-Louis Barye*, London, 1926

Shepherd Gallery, The, *Western European Bronzes of the 19th Century*, USA, 1972

JEWELRY

Cooper, Diana and Norman Battershill, *Victorian Sentimental Jewellery*, Devon, 1972

Flower, Margaret, *Victorian Jewellery*, London, 1967

Gere, Charlotte, *Victorian Jewellery Design*, London, 1970

Peter, Mary, *Collecting Victorian Jewellery*, London, 1970

SILVER & METALWORK

Blair, Claude, *The History of Silver*, New York, 1987

Bury, Shirley, *Victorian Electroplate*, London, 1971

Hughes, G. Bernard, *Small Antique Silverware (including flatware)*, London, 1957

Wardle, Patricia, *Victorian Silver and Silver-Plate*, London, 1963

TEXTILES

Godden, G.A., *Stevengraphs and other Victorian Silk Pictures*, London, 1971

Morris, Barbara, *Victorian Embroidery*, London, 1962

MISCELLANEOUS

Melvin, Andrew, *William Morris: wallpapers and designs*, London, 1971

Pinto, Edward, *Treen and other Wooden Bygones*, London, 1969

Pinto, Edward and Eva, *Tunbridge and Scottish Souvenir Woodware*, London, 1970

INDEX

187

PICTURE CREDITS AND ACKNOWLEDGMENTS

The publishers would like to thank the following auction houses, museums, dealers, collectors and other sources for supplying pictures for use in this book or for allowing their pieces to be photographed.

1 SL; 3 SL; 5 Sil; 12 SL; 14 CL; 15l&rt CL; 15rb MB; 16 SL; 17(x2) SL; 18 FAS; 19t SL; 19b CL; 20 B; 21t SL; 21b CL; 22 CL; 23t CL; 23bl&r SL; 24t CL; 24b SL; 25 CL; 26 SL; 27l MB; 27r SL; 28 SL; 29t SL; 29(x3) SL; 30 V&A; 31(x2) CE; 32 CNY; 33(x3) B&B; 34 CL; 36 MB; 37(x2) MB; 38 SL; 39t SNY; 39bl SL; 39br MB; 40 PC; 41(x2) PC; 42 EK/MB; 43t MB; 43bl MB; 43br SL; 44 SL; 45 t row SL; 45 2nd row (x2) SL; 45 3rd row SNY; 45 4th and b row SL; 46 P; 47t P; 47c CL; 47b P; 48 CL; 49(x3) CL; 50 Cor; 51(x2) Cor; 52 MB; 54 MB; 55(x2) MB; 56 SL; 57l SL; 57r MB; 58 MB; 59(x2) MB; 60 SL; 61l SL; 61r EK/MB; 62 SL; 63(x2) MB; 64 MB; 65(x2) RD; 66 SL; 67t LG; 67b SL; 68 DB; 69(x2) SL; 70 CE; 71tl,bl SL; 71tr&br MB; 72 SL; 73t,br SL; 73bl MB; 74 SL; 75(x2) CL; 76 MB; 77tl CL; 77tr MB; 77b JL; 78 Tor; 79(x3) Tor; 80 CL; 81(x2) CL; 82 MB; 83t MB; 83b P; 84 CL; 85t CL; 85c&b SL; 86 RD; 87(x3) RD: 88 CL; 89t&b CL; 89c Wil; 90 DL; 91(x2) RdR; 92 Sil; 93(x3) Sil; 94 CNY; 95(x2) CNY; 96 B; 98 SL; 99t&c SL; 99b FAS; 100(x2) SL; 101(x3) SL; 102(x2) SL; 103(x3) SL; 104 SL; 105t SL; 105b FAS; 106 SL; 107(x2) SL; 108 B; 109l&br SL; 109tr CL; 110 SL; 111(x2) SL; 112 CSK; 114 CSK; 115(x4) CSK; 116 CSK; 117(x5) CSK; 118 CSK; 119(x3) CSK; 120(x2) CSK; 121(x4) CSK; 122 RJS; 123 TC; 124 SL; 126 RP/MB; 127(x2) MB; 128 CL; 129l SL; 129tr MB; 129br SL; 130 CL; 131(x2) CL; 132 CL; 133(x3) SL; 134 CL; 135 SL; 136 H&W; 137t MB; 137b(x2) CL; 138 CNY; 139(x2) CNY; 140l(x2) CL; 140tr MB; 140br SL; 141tl SF/MB; 141tr MB; 141lc&lb B; 141b SF/MB; 142 PC; 144 V&A; 145(x2) PC; 146 PC; 147tl&br PC; 147bl SL; 148 PC; 149t&bl PC; 149br P; 150 PC; 151(x3) PC; 152t WF; 152b WAG; 153l WF; 153r PC; 154 SL; 155l V&A; 155r SL; 156 WAG; 157l PC; 157r WAG; 158 CNY; 159(x2) CNY; 160 MB; 162t&c SL; 162b B; 163tl P(C); 163tr P; 163b B; 164(x2) SF/MB; 165 tl&r(x2) SF/MB; 165b MB; 166(x2) SF/MB; 167(x3) SF/MB; 168(x3) BEB; 169tl B; 169tr,bl&br CSK; 170l SL; 170r SF/MB; 171tl MB; 171tr SF/MB; 171bl MB; 172 l SF/MB; 172tr SF/MB; 172br BEB; 173l(x2) B; 173tr FF; 173rc EHA; 173rb SF/MB; 174(x2) SNY; 175t CNY; 175b SNY; jacket SNY.

KEY

b bottom, c centre, l left, r right, t top

B	Bonham's, London	P	Phillips, London
B & B	Butterfield & Butterfield, Los Angeles	PC	Private Collection
		P(C)	Phillips, Cardiff
BEB	Judith Bebber	RD	Richard Dennis, Ilminster
CE	Christie's East	RdR	Rogers de Rin Antiques, London
CL	Christie's, London		
CNY	Christie's, New York	RJS	Ruth and Joseph Sataloff
Cor	Corning Museum of Glass, New York	RP	Richard Price
		Sil	Dr and Mrs Howard Silby
CSK	Christie's, South Kensington	SF/MB	Stephen Furniss, Asters Antiques, Shere, Surrey
DB	David Battie	SL	Sotheby's, London
DL	Dr Laird	SNY	Sotheby's, New York
EHA	Gloria Gibson	TC	Tiffany Collection/ Stephen B. Leek
EK	Eric Knowles		
FAS	The Fine Art Society, London	Tor	Torquay Pottery Collectors Society
		V&A	Victoria & Albert Museum, London
FF	Fan-Fayre		
H&W	Haslam & Whiteway Ltd, London	WAG	Whitworth Art Gallery, Manchester
JL	Jocelyn Lukins	WF	Warner Fabrics, PLC
LG	L Greengrass, Stow-on-the-Wold	Wil	Williamson Art Gallery, Birkenhead
MB	Mitchell Beazley		